GENERATION Z LEARNS

—

*A Guide for Engaging Generation Z
Students in Meaningful Learning*

Corey Seemiller and Meghan Grace

ISBN-13: 9781092872416

CONTENTS

About the Authors ·ix
About the Book ·xi
Introduction · xiii

1   Learning Today · 1
Information Overload · 1
   Searchable Terms · 2
   Class Repository · 3
Credible Information · 3
   Credible Sources · 4
   Rationale Sheet · 5
   Unlearning · 6
Critical Thinking · 7
   Point-Counterpoint · 8
   Self-Debate · 9
Creativity · 9
   From Traditional to Creative Expressions · · · · · · 10
   Innovative Presentations · · · · · · · · · · · · · · · · · 10
   Class Facilitation · 11

Digital Portfolios · 12

Attention Spans · 13

Unplugging · 13

Taking a Break · 14

Mindfulness · 14

Summary · 15

2   The Role of Family and Friends in Learning · · · · · 17

Families · 17

Learning is Close to Home · · · · · · · · · · · · · · · 19

Familial Connection, Reflection, and Application · · 19

Inviting in Family · 20

Friends and Peers · 20

Capitalizing on Peer Influence · · · · · · · · · · · · · 21

Peer Role Models · 22

Summary · 22

3   The Learners · 23

Characteristics and Strengths · · · · · · · · · · · · · · · 23

Leveraging Their Potential · · · · · · · · · · · · · · · · 24

Motivations · 24

Relational Motivation Strategies · · · · · · · · · · · · 25

Achievement Motivation Strategies · · · · · · · · · · 26

Feeling Stressed · 28

Stress Management · 28

Summary · 29

4   The Instructors · 31

Characteristics and Behaviors · · · · · · · · · · · · · · · 32

Being Engaging and Enthusiastic · · · · · · · · · · · 32

Having Passion · 32

Demonstrating Humor and Wit · · · · · · · · · · · · 33

Possessing Knowledge and Experience · · · · · · · · · 34

Discussing the Difficulty of Learning · · · · · · · · 34

Communication, Connection, and Interaction · · · · 35

Fostering Connections · 35

Communicating Face-to-Face · · · · · · · · · · · · · · 36

Texting · 36

Emailing · 37

Students Not Wanting to Disappoint · · · · · · · · · · · 41

Building Authentic Relationships · · · · · · · · · · · 42

Fueling Intrinsic Motivation · · · · · · · · · · · · · · · 42

Summary · 43

5   The Learning Environment · · · · · · · · · · · · · · · · · 45

Quiet Setting · 46

Soothing Sounds or None at All · · · · · · · · · · · · 46

Ideal Learning Spaces · 47

Creating an Ideal Learning Environment · · · · · 48

Taking it Outside · 49

Finding Comfortable Campus Nooks · · · · · · · · 50

Helping Students Develop Healthy Boundaries
with Devices · 50

Setting Expectations · 52

Sharing Research on Digital Distractions · · · · · 53

Offering Engaging Instruction · · · · · · · · · · · · · 53

Helping Students Manage Boundaries with
Personal Devices · 54

Incorporating Personal Devices in Class · · · · · · 55

Summary · 55

6   Instructional Design · 57

Intrapersonal Learning · 57

    Structuring Choice · 59

    Pacing the Learning · 60

    Offering Space for Multiple Interpretation · · · · · 61

    Flipping the Learning · 61

    Building Confidence · 63

    Teaching One-on-One · 64

Social Learning · 65

    Hybrid Over Online Courses · · · · · · · · · · · · · · 66

    Peer Support and Assistance · · · · · · · · · · · · · · · 67

Experiential Learning · 67

    Interactive Activities · 68

    Peer Learning · 68

Demonstrated Learning · 68

    Demonstrations · 69

Digital Learning · 70

    Video-Based Learning · 70

    Engaging Apps and Platforms · · · · · · · · · · · · · · 70

    The Role of Social Media in Learning · · · · · · · · 71

Summary · 73

7   Content · 75

Emotional Intelligence · 75

    Incorporating Social and Emotional
Learning in K–12 · 76

    Infusing Emotional Intelligence Across the
College Curriculum · 76

Success Skills · 77

    Enhancing Skills for Academic Success · · · · · · · · 78

Life and Career Application · · · · · · · · · · · · · · · · · 78
  Bringing in Real-Life Scenarios · · · · · · · · · · · · · 78
  Enhancing Professional Skills · · · · · · · · · · · · · · 79
  Helping Them Help Others· · · · · · · · · · · · · · · · 80
Social Change· 80
  Helping Them Discover and Articulate
  Their Passions · 81
  From Service Learning to Social
  Change Learning· 82
  Summary · 85

8   Assignments · 87
    The Role of Reading· 87
      Amount of Reading· 88
      Focusing Reading · 89
      Integrating Everyday Readings · · · · · · · · · · · · 89
      Incorporating Interactive Consumable Content · · · 90
      Utilizing Traditional Reading Formats · · · · · · · · 90
      Maintaining Standards of Reading
      Accountability· 91
    Defining Assignment Expectations · · · · · · · · · · · · 91
      Sharing Intent Behind Assignments· · · · · · · · · · 92
      Providing Clear Instructions · · · · · · · · · · · · · · 92
      Sharing Model Assignments · · · · · · · · · · · · · · 93
    Group Work · 93
      Group Project Formation· · · · · · · · · · · · · · · · · 95
      Group Development · 97
      Team Contracts· 97
      Mandatory Group Meeting · · · · · · · · · · · · · · · 98
      Work Distribution · 99

Individual Contributions · · · · · · · · · · · · · · · · · · 100
Accountability Standards· · · · · · · · · · · · · · · · · 101
Milestones · 101
Dividing Up Large Assignments · · · · · · · · · · · 102
Gamification · 102
Providing Feedback· 103
Timely, Thorough, and Ongoing Feedback · · · · 104
Observational Feedback· · · · · · · · · · · · · · · · · · 104
General Performance Feedback · · · · · · · · · · · · 105
Opportunities to Integrate Feedback · · · · · · · · 105
Summary · 106

Conclusion · 107
Acknowledgments· 109
Notes · 111
References· 133
Index · 147

About the Authors

COREY SEEMILLER, PhD, is a faculty member at Wright State University in the Department of Leadership Studies in Education and Organizations. She has taught at the college level for over twenty years and has researched and published on issues related to teaching and learning. Dr. Seemiller earned her PhD in higher education from the University of Arizona, is the author of *The Student Leadership Competencies Guidebook* and associated tools and resources, and is the coauthor of *Generation Z Goes to College, Generation Z Leads,* and *Generation Z: A Century in the Making.*

MEGHAN GRACE is an associate with Plaid LLC. She has served in both campus-based and organizational roles in the areas of leadership development, program and event planning, assessment, and fraternity and sorority programs. Meghan earned her MA degree in higher education from the University of Arizona. She is the coauthor of *Generation Z Goes to College, Generation Z Leads,* and *Generation Z: A Century in the Making.*

ABOUT THE BOOK

This book is the fourth in a series about the post-Millennial generation, Generation Z. As this generational cohort comprises students from elementary school through graduate school, having a better understanding of them can be helpful for anyone in a formal or informal educational role working with this population.

This book includes findings from our two major studies, the 2014 *Generation Z Goes to College* study and the 2017 *Generation Z Stories* study. Information on these studies can be found on our website at www.thegenzhub.com. We also include findings from several other studies and reports that offer critical information for understanding the characteristics and learning preferences of this generation.

The following chapters cover topics such as learning today, the role of family and friends in learning, the learners, the instructors, the learning environment, course design, pedagogy, content, and assignments. In addition to offering insight into this generation, several Generation Z-friendly teaching and learning strategies and practices are discussed.

INTRODUCTION

Born 1995 through 2010, Generation Z students are the primary student population in our classrooms—from elementary school to graduate school. Yet we are still learning about this generation and who these individuals are as students. We do know that members of Generation Z possess characteristics, including thoughtfulness and compassion, reflective of the role they play in relationships and are motivated by the impact they have on others.[1] They seek careers that provide enjoyment and happiness, fulfillment, passion, and greater meaning, with the ultimate goal of wanting to make a positive impact through their work.[2] But there is much more to discover about this generation as we aim to effectively leverage their capacities and foster their potential in our classrooms and institutions altogether.

1

LEARNING TODAY

Education today may look much like it did fifty years ago—classrooms, lesson plans, textbooks, and course assignments. In many ways, not much appears to have changed. Even so, access to new information, pedagogies, courses, facilities, programs, and technology has influenced the development of an educational landscape unique to this era. To better understand who our Generation Z learners are today, it is important to uncover contemporary contextual factors that can affect their learning. Five critical areas discussed in this chapter include information overload, credible information, critical thinking, creativity, and attention spans.

INFORMATION OVERLOAD
The internet has provided an unparalleled opportunity for everyday people to create and disseminate information in vast quantities, more so than ever before. It was not too long

ago that writing book reports involved looking up a topic in a set of encyclopedias and drafting a summary of the one source. Today, there can be hundreds, and even thousands, of web pages overviewing a topic. And it seems like just yesterday students were trying to find that one journal article with exactly the information they needed, only to go to the library and find the journal issue had been misplaced and was nowhere to be found. Today, students do not even need to go to a library or open a hard-copy book to research and write papers. Nearly all students today are researching information for assignments by going online.[3] Our "fast-paced and flattened world"[4] allows students to be just a few clicks away from finding more information than they could ever need, and sometimes more than is actually helpful. A study of teachers found that 83 percent believe "the amount of information available online today is overwhelming to most students."[5]

While we can tell students there is more than enough information out there to complete their assignments, it is important to remember that information overload can also cause a saturation in which it becomes challenging to sift through vast amounts of potentially irrelevant information simply to find the content needed.

SEARCHABLE TERMS

Because there is so much information available today, some teachers believe that students think they can find information easily online without having to put in a great deal of effort.[6] But students quickly realize they end up with a lot of extraneous information if they do not know how to effectively engage in online research. One way to help students traverse this landscape of information overload is to provide a lesson on how to develop search terms to help them find the information they are seeking more efficiently. Sometimes, students will put specific phrases into a search engine and come up with little, which may lead them to think there is nothing available on their topic. However, a short tutorial covering strategies such as using synonyms, search suggestions on Google, options at the top of the page (such as web, images, etc.) to filter information, a hyphen to exclude words, or putting quotation marks around exact phrases,[7] can be useful in helping students effectively engage in online research.

CLASS REPOSITORY
Another option to help with information overload is to provide a class repository of links to readings, videos, and educational resources that have been vetted by the instructor to ensure there is enough information available to adequately complete an assignment. Then students would only need to sort through a finite number of preselected sources to find appropriate information while learning more about what constitutes credible and quality resources.

CREDIBLE INFORMATION
In 2001, Wikipedia was born.[8] The new platform was designed to serve as a user-written and user-edited online encyclopedia.[9] Because Wikipedia launched in the early 2000s, Millennial students were some of the first to look to

it as an informative source, some citing it as a reference for research in and of itself. By 2009, the American Psychological Association put forth recommendations for when and when not to cite Wikipedia as a reference and suggested using the listed citations to link directly to original scholarly research.[10]

Instructors have been struggling to figure out if and how Wikipedia fits into their students' research endeavors, and they now also have to contend with students getting information from social media rather than scholarly databases.[11] In an increasingly user-generated digital world, students may look to citing blogs, op-eds, and personal websites. Because the internet provides access to more information, instructors and learners are now faced with sifting through and sorting out what is credible. And with 37 percent of Generation Z college seniors having reported they either never or only occasionally evaluate the quality or reliability of the information they receive, it appears that much work is to be done helping students of all ages learn to assess the credibility of content.[12]

CREDIBLE SOURCES

It is imperative to do two things in a culture where credibility is not always a given. First, there is a need to continue to educate students on what constitutes a legitimate source. This may take place in a writing or English course, a library workshop, or a first-year college seminar. And while students may have been taught this one time, it is critical that credibility of content be discussed across the curriculum as students move from grade to grade in K–12 and course to course in higher education.

Second, it is important to infuse education on credible sources across the entire program curriculum. Program faculty may need to work together to find a place in one or more of the earlier program courses to include content on determining the credibility of sources. The content may be scaffolded so that while it is not repeated in subsequent courses, it is reiterated, reinforced, and refined to reflect the applicability for higher-level courses.

RATIONALE SHEET

Another way to help students assess the credibility of sources is to have them investigate references. Have students submit a rationale sheet that describes why each reference was included in a particular assignment. Or, further, ask them to submit a credibility analysis on each source that includes a short biography of the author, process for publication, and background of the publication source (values, perspectives, funding streams, etc.). Students would then analyze the credibility of the source using the information they found.

Another approach involves having students complete a checklist to assess the credibility of each reference.[13] The following is a sample checklist:

- The purpose of this article is educational and not commercial, promotional, or for entertainment.
- The content is based on cited research rather than opinion or anecdotal evidence.

- The author has the experience, credentials, or both to be writing as an authority on this topic.
- All claims or arguments in the article are supported by references.
- There is a reference list at the end of the article.
- The article is current enough to be applied to a contemporary issue.
- The platform where this article is located is current, and the web links to other pages are functioning.
- The article does not appear to omit counterarguments obvious to the everyday reader.

And with practice, students may eventually learn to use these criteria without having to refer to the checklist.

UNLEARNING

With technology at our fingertips and user-generated content being uploaded continuously, information is far more abundant and accessible for students today than it was in the past. But this information is not always accurate. The primary role of an educator has always been helping students learn. But in more recent years, that role has expanded to also helping students learn how to learn.[14] And now instructors must also help students unlearn misinformation they bring into the learning environment. How can this unlearning process be done? Consider having an assignment in which students are asked to write about what they know on a subject without researching it. This can help the instructor assess the accuracy of their knowledge of the subject matter. To build on that exercise, students would then research the subject matter and compare and contrast what they thought they knew with what might be correct.

CRITICAL THINKING

Another contextual factor of today's learning landscape involves the ability, ease, and even allure, to find a quick answer, even if it is not the correct one or the best one.[15] In an effort to get an assignment done before the deadline, some Generation Z students may go online and take the first quote, statistic, or piece of seemingly related content that emerges from the search. Taking information from the web at face value even if it appears to be inconsistent with their experiences or instincts may be due to students not giving themselves enough time to research a topic fully and adequately. More importantly, taking information at face value may be indicative of a need for students to engage in critical thinking, which involves the "analysis and assessment of information about a subject in order to reach an objective judgment."[16]

With so much information available, assignments can simply become fill-in-the-blank exercises in which students select a topic and angle and then find the first available data point to populate into the assignment to support their position. Consider it like Mad Libs, which asks the participant to fill in a verb or noun to complete an already written sentence. Being able to find nearly any information online that supports any viewpoint makes it easy to just search for a quote that says *X* or a statistic that demonstrates *Y*.

Today, society needs graduates who are able to come up with innovative and creative solutions to solve the complex issues facing society.[17] The World Economic Forum listed critical thinking as the second most essential competency for the 2020 workforce.[18] In addition, 92 percent of teachers of sixth through twelfth graders said that developing critical thinking skills should be a priority.[19] Yet only 81 percent of sixth through twelfth graders in the same study said they were learning those skills in school.[20] There was also a gap between the 93 percent of teachers who indicated that solving real-world problems should be an educational priority compared to just 69 percent of students who noted having engaged in developing real-world problem-solving skills in school.[21] At the college level, the numbers also point to an overall lack of students readily using critical thinking skills. Although nearly 59 percent of Generation Z college seniors say they frequently try to find alternative solutions to problems, the other 41 percent either never do or only do occasionally.[22] It appears that there is a clear need to help students at all educational levels develop the capacity to look at multiple viewpoints to make informed assessments and generate conclusions.

POINT-COUNTERPOINT
One recommendation to help students engage in critical thinking would be to have them use a point-counterpoint approach in which they are asked to include counterpoints

to all their sources. This might appear as two conflicting research findings or points of view. Doing so would require students to research multiple sides of a topic while at the same time engaging in deeper research to find content that would support both sides.

SELF-DEBATE

Another idea to enhance critical thinking with students is to ask them to learn about a particular side of an issue (e.g. making recycling mandatory). This can simply be an informal task in which they research data and information during class, or a more formal assignment, such as completing a paper or a presentation outside of class. After the students have researched the issue, ask each student to either write or verbally discuss three valid points reflective of an opposing viewpoint related to the issue in their assignment (e.g. keeping recycling voluntary). Not only can this exercise be insightful to better understand how holistically the students understand the assigned issue, but it can also point out to students how easy it is to only seek out information that supports one point of view.

CREATIVITY

The World Economic Forum listed creativity as the third most essential skill needed by employers by 2020.[23] Many of the youngest of those in Generation Z, and subsequently Generation Alpha, are now utilizing makerspaces and design labs in their schools. And with the recent notion that STEAM might simply be more robust than STEM, schools today are focusing more on the arts.[24]

However, 45 percent of Generation Z college seniors believe their level of creativity is at or below average.[25] Of course, many in this generational cohort experienced cuts to time spent on art and music during their K–12 schooling.[26] And today, 76 percent of sixth through twelfth grade students and 75 percent of their teachers wish there was more of a focus on creativity in the curriculum.[27] So how do instructors develop, embrace, and utilize creativity with this generation at all levels of schooling, especially with older students who may not have had as many opportunities for enhancing their creativity?

FROM TRADITIONAL TO CREATIVE EXPRESSIONS

Some types of assignments, such as papers and reports, appear to have stood the test of time. But might there be a more creative way for students to demonstrate their learning of a particular subject matter that is outside the bounds of traditional homework? For example, instead of a research paper, students could complete a 3-D model or instead of a case study report, they could perform a theatrical performance.

INNOVATIVE PRESENTATIONS

We know that both instructors and students rely on PowerPoint slides for presentations. But challenging students to use varying presentation formats and platforms for the slides could tap into their creative minds. One example is the Pecha Kucha, which is a timed presentation comprised of twenty slides at twenty seconds each, totaling 640 seconds.[28] Students are asked to divide their presentation into twenty slides with twenty seconds' worth of talking points for each. Each slide needs to include only an image that is associated with a designated talking point. This presentation style helps students think creatively about what they can say in twenty-second timed increments as well as not read from text-heavy slides.

Instead of PowerPoint slides altogether, another idea is to have students design presentations with an engaging twist. One such way is by using a platform called Powtoon. This site allows users to design cartoon characters that act out content. Not only can these types of presentations be fun to make, but they are also interesting to watch, especially as students try to think creatively of ways to integrate their content into a cartoon format.

In addition, perhaps reducing or eliminating the use of technology altogether can help students tap into their creative selves. For instance, the TED model of 9–15 minutes of memorized content could provide students a means to think creatively about how they want to tell a story.[29]

CLASS FACILITATION

Another method to help students develop creativity centers on class facilitation. Having students facilitate a discussion or activity during class can create a means for helping students think about inventive ways to engage their peers. Students could develop discussion prompts, role-plays, or case studies, requiring them to think more creatively about both the content and the process for teaching it.

DIGITAL PORTFOLIOS

Another means for infusing creativity into the classroom involves incorporating a digital learning portfolio. Digital portfolios are essentially personal websites where students can showcase themselves and their work to an external audience, which could include prospective employers, college or graduate school admissions officers, or selection committees for scholarships or awards. Some educators use digital portfolios as repositories for their assessment of the students' collection of learning artifacts, however, the focus of using digital portfolios as personal websites is instead to have students develop a forward-facing digital showcase of themselves to share with an external audience.

Digital portfolios can be housed on many website builders such as Wix or Weebly. To create a digital portfolio, students would obtain a personal account on a website builder and start developing pages and content. In addition, some sites are designed specifically for creating digital portfolios, such as Adobe Portfolio. Various learning management systems also integrate digital portfolios. However, it is important that students are able to access their portfolio after leaving school, which often is not the case for learning management system portfolios. Thus, it is important to research various platforms to select a tool best suited for the learning situation.

While the digital portfolio can include any component required by the instructor, some common components include students' sample work, personal mission and vision statements, educational and career goals, educational or professional credentials and certificates, and descriptions of co-curricular, volunteer, and work experience. With digital portfolios, students can define their personal brand by selecting colors, fonts, and images, as well as design the layout and choose a personal tag line.

ATTENTION SPANS

Over the last 10 years, attention spans of individuals have decreased from twelve minutes to five minutes.[30] This does not seem surprising considering how easy is it to flip and swipe through news stories in milliseconds, have multiple tabs open on one device, or even have Netflix on in the background while surfing the web, texting on a smartwatch, and scrolling through social media feeds. In a study of digital distractions, 58 percent of Generation Z college students reported engaging in online activities unrelated to school while studying.[31] Given these factors, consider the following options for helping students manage their academic work during an era of declining attention spans.

UNPLUGGING

One option involves having students disabling or disconnecting the wireless connection on their phones both during classes and while they are studying. This can reduce the temptation for the student to "just check a message quickly." But if that is too much, simply having students turn off notifications, badge icons, and automatic feeds that populate messages on a locked screen can be a big help. This can be done by adjusting notifications in the phone settings or even enabling the phone's do-not-disturb function either manually or set on a pre-programmed timer just for class or study time. Doing so can eliminate the pressing need students may feel when they see an app notification pop up or an actual message on the home screen. But it is important to not simply require or suggest these ideas. In a world of FOMO (or *fear of missing out*), there may not be a good time in students' minds to unplug.[32] So having conversations with them about why unplugging can be beneficial may ease the anxiety of being disconnected.

TAKING A BREAK

Research has found that brains engage in rest-activity cycles that start over after 90 minutes.[33] Thus, encouraging students to take a break from studying or school work after 90 minutes could give them a refreshed and renewed sense of focus.[34] Maybe a quick walk, technology break to check messages, or just getting up and getting a snack can do wonders for getting refocused again.

MINDFULNESS

But contending with short attention spans is not solely related to fighting the allure of constant digital connection. There are other means of helping students enhance their ability to focus. For example, mindfulness, meditation, and attention-focused activities have been found to increase one's sense of focus and decrease the level of mind wandering.[35] Thus, offering campus programs and services on mindfulness could have an impact on attention spans in the classroom and when studying. In addition, engaging in activities such as exercising and playing video games as well as avoiding multitasking can help reduce students' ability to be easily distracted.[36] And while these activities might not be conducive to the classroom environment, encouraging students to engage in these types of activities on their own time may have educational benefits.

While there may be limited resources on the part of the institution to offer freestanding mindfulness programs or students may be too busy to attend out-of-class experiences, it might be useful to find ways to include mindfulness in the classroom curriculum. Engaging students in quiet reflection, visualization, or deep breathing could be a great way to start or end class.

SUMMARY

Today's cultural and social landscape has impacted student learning in ways we are still uncovering. But what is known is that information overload, the difficulty in finding and assessing the credibility of information, challenges in critical thinking, a need for more creativity in the curriculum, and declining attention spans are issues that must be recognized and considered by instructors as they design learning experiences. Doing so may help maximize the learning potential of Generation Z students.

2

The Role of Family and Friends in Learning

Generation Z is a very relationally focused generation,[37] with families and friends playing a significant role in the lives of many of these young people. Whether the students want to consult these important individuals or simply keep them informed, their inner circles are significant to Generation Z students' learning.

Families

When Gen Xers were in college, 29 percent identified their parents as their number one role model.[38] This may not be surprising because Gen Xers were often referred to as latch-key kids due to having both parents in the workforce,[39] perhaps influencing the extent to which they saw their parents as their primary role models. By the time Millennials came to campus, the number who saw their parents as their number one role models increased to 54 percent.[40] For those in Generation Z, the number jumped even higher to 69 percent.[41]

But this differentiation between the numbers of Millennials and members of Generation Z who see their parents as their primary role models are not explained by the extent parents are involved in their day-to-day lives. For example, parents of Millennials have often been referred to as "helicopter parents" for hovering so closely over their kids and solving problems for them.[42] And while the notion of lawnmower or snowplow parents of Generation Z has emerged in the media, the evidence of such behavior on a wide scale is sparse and tied more specifically to upper-income parents providing monetary support to their children.[43] Other non-financial measures associated with lawnmower parenting, such as giving adult children romantic or professional advice or engaging in frequent communication, may simply be reflective of the mentorship role that parents play for Generation Z students.

Instead, intrusive parenting appears to be less of an issue with those in Generation Z than Millennials. For example, far fewer Generation Z students indicated having received help on their homework from their parents compared to Millennials.[44] And many parents of Generation Z are not likely to intervene in their children's education to solve a problem or talk to an instructor for them. These parents are instead instilling in their kids the importance of independence and self-reliance,[45] reinforcing the notion that actions have consequences.[46]

Providing autonomy does not necessarily mean that the parents of Generation Z students are detached from their children's lives. Incidentally, two-thirds of Gen Xers feel closer to their Generation Z children than they did with their own parents.[47] The perception of closeness with their children is not just in the eyes of the Gen X parents. Eighty-eight percent of those in Generation Z say their relationships with their parents are extremely close,[48] and 89 percent believe their parents have the largest influence on their personal values.[49] Thus, Generation Z's parents have been dubbed co-pilots for the collaborative role their children have invited them to partake in when it comes to their own decision-making.[50] Interestingly, for many Generation Z students, their Gen X parents who did not see their own parents as their primary role models have now become role models for their Generation Z children.

Learning is Close to Home

Given their close connections with parents, it would make sense that learning should feel close to home. For example, instead of having students interview someone they do not know for an assignment, have them interview someone they do know. Or, rather than provide case study scenarios, have students develop their own scenarios based on their real-life experiences. This is a generation that highly trusts and is influenced by people close to them.[51, 52] Because of that, they may be more apt to relate to the experiences of those in their inner circles.

Familial Connection, Reflection, and Application

Because parents and families are incredibly important to most Generation Z students, some discuss details of assignments, projects, and courses with them, thus supporting the co-pilot mentality.[53] Their close parental relationships are likely not going away when they enter the classroom or enroll in college. What then can instructors do to help students connect their learning and their family lives? Consider introducing reflection prompts related to one's family or inner circle where the student reflects on how course concepts apply to their families and loved ones. Or have students make meaning of the course content by looking through the lens of the experiences, philosophies, and values of their family members. Incorporating families into the curriculum allows students to integrate those they care so deeply about into their everyday academic lives.

INVITING IN FAMILY

Another way to embrace the important role that families play in the lives of Generation Z students involves inviting the families into the course. For example, consider having students give their final presentations, show a short film, give a demonstration, or read a poem at an end-of-the-semester evening event where families are invited. While this may happen with younger students more readily, incorporating this approach with older (even college) students could have its benefits.

FRIENDS AND PEERS

Friends and peers also play an important role in the lives of Generation Z students. Second, only to their parents, friends are the number one shapers of Generation Z values,[54] and peers are highly influential in what their friends determine is cool.[55] This might not seem shocking, as the influence of friends and peers has been around long before these students were even born. It is, however, interesting to note that in a world where social media influencers, celebrities, and others in the digital world have so much direct access to young people that their inner circles are still the most influential.

CAPITALIZING ON PEER INFLUENCE

Peer feedback can be a useful learning tool. When students receive feedback, they can use that information to improve their own assignments and work. Further, though, students who provide feedback can gain insight into their own work by comparing their assignment to another student's assignment.[56]

One way to integrate a peer feedback process includes partnering up students at the beginning of the semester to serve as each other's assignment reviewer. Then, each time an assignment is due, the student is required to submit the assignment with a copy reviewed by their partner. This ensures that the student receives critical feedback that can help in improving the final version of their assignment.

But how do we help students give effective feedback rather than simply glossing over the paper and saying "good job" when there are clearly spelling errors and grammatical issues? It may be useful at the beginning of the semester to go over how to effectively provide peer feedback on assignments; describing what to look for and having them practice with sample work. Further, providing a reviewer checklist with items related to grammar, flow, organization, references, and structure provides students a guide to use when reviewing others' work.

PEER ROLE MODELS

Given the influence peers have on this generation, Generation Z students would likely be eager to take advice and learn from their peers. For example, having undergraduate preceptors, proctors, or teaching assistants in a college classroom could offer a formalized and structured way to incorporate peer learning. Students then have someone who they can directly relate to serving as their guide for academic success. In addition, having more senior students who previously took a class to assist current students or even peers who are not in the same class or classes can serve as useful mentors for Generation Z students as they navigate their educational experiences.

In addition, while it may be nothing new to pull in current students or recent alumni to present, serve as guest speakers, or mentor current students, it is still a valuable practice to use with Generation Z students. Learning directly from their peers' experience could be eye-opening for this young generation as they realize that their closeness in age may provide a more relatable reflection of their anticipated experience than the stories told by their older instructors.

SUMMARY

It is important to consider that the inner circles of Generation Z students are highly influential in their lives. And their educational experience is no exception. As instructors, integrating family members and friends into a course could help students connect better with the material and feel a sense of real-life application.

3

THE LEARNERS

Today's education context has some nuances that differentiate it from even a generation ago. Likewise, Generation Z learners are different as well. Their characteristics and strengths, motivations, and overwhelming sense of stress are unique to their generational cohort and may affect the way instructors need to approach teaching.

CHARACTERISTICS AND STRENGTHS

When asked to identify characteristics that describe them, over 70 percent of Generation Z students selected loyal, thoughtful, determined, compassionate, open-minded, and responsible.[57] These characteristics point to a learner who is open to new ideas, works hard, and follows through on their work. Our more recent research also indicates that this is a generation of young people who demonstrate great loyalty and care for others as well as a sense of responsibility to themselves and others.[58] And their independent[59] and self-reliant[60]

Gen X parents might have helped to instill these qualities in them.

In addition to the general characteristics of Generation Z students, the VIA Institute on Character's dataset reveals that the most commonly reported top five strengths of members of this generation include honesty, kindness, humor, fairness, and judgment.[61] It appears that their honesty, fairness, and judgment may be related to their characteristics of loyalty, determination, and responsibility. And their kindness and humor might be connected to their thoughtfulness, compassion, and open-mindedness. Together, we see a determined, yet caring, generation of learners. These characteristics and strengths point to students who want to learn, not give up, and strive to help others.

LEVERAGING THEIR POTENTIAL

We can perhaps see the prominent characteristics and strengths of Generation Z not just related to how they approach their learning but also as the key to their learning. Tapping into their sense of responsibility could help get them over the finish line to complete an assignment. In addition, leveraging their compassion and kindness could help them when working with groups, and encouraging open-mindedness might empower them to seek out alternative views to expand their learning.

MOTIVATIONS

Much research has been done over the decades linking motivation and academic success.[62] Thus, as instructors, we want our students to be motivated to learn. In our *Generation Z Goes to College* study, we found that Generation Z students are motivated more for relational reasons than for those related to individual reward. For example, three-quarters indicated being motivated by not wanting to let others down, knowing that their actions will make a difference for someone, and advocating for something they believe in.[63] All of these types of motivations draw from a sense of responsibility for others or causes that may impact others—reflecting their relationship-oriented characteristics and strengths. In addition, 74 percent are motivated by knowing they would receive credit for their contribution or as an opportunity for advancement, reflecting a desire for achievement.[64] How can instructors leverage Generation Z students' motivation preferences around relationships and achievement to help them capitalize on their learning?

RELATIONAL MOTIVATION STRATEGIES

This is a generation that holds kindness, fairness, and compassion close to their hearts.[65,66] It is no surprise that most are motivated by their relationships and the impact they have on others. Thus, some key ideas to integrate when it comes to learning must involve the effect of their behavior on other people. For example, emphasizing to a student that their lack of involvement can have a negative effect on their group members may help get students to take a more active role in a group project.

Attendance, especially in higher education where students can opt to not come to class, may be affected by a student's motivation. Helping students understand that being absent does not only mean that other students would miss out on their insights (which surely is relational) but that the content the students miss could be crucial to effectively doing their jobs in the future. Not knowing how to do something or doing it ineffectively might have real-life implications on people. For example, missing a class session where the topic is a specific computer programming platform could result in later not coding something properly in a job, ultimately affecting platform users. Instructors can share the implications for missing class or even ask students to generate a list of what they might not learn if they missed a certain class session.

In addition, this is a generation of students who care deeply about ensuring they do not let others down.[67] Not performing to the best of their ability or not giving 100 percent in school could ultimately let down their friends and family who may be providing financial, logistical, or emotional support for them in their educational pursuits.

ACHIEVEMENT MOTIVATION STRATEGIES

In addition to being motivated by impacting others, Generation Z students are motivated by working toward an achievement.[68] For example, they may strive to complete an assignment because the points they earn will ultimately contribute to their overall grade. Messages such as, "This paper is worth 30 percent of your grade," can help frame individual pieces of the course in a larger context.

Students may also be motivated knowing that completing a course allows them to check off a requirement for educational advancement. A message that might resonate well with them is, "We are halfway through the course already." This is a generation that appreciates knowing that the hard work they are putting forth today can also result in something bigger later on.[69] For example, for college students, it could be very motivating to be told that doing well in a particular prerequisite course will position them better for all of the specialty courses in the major later on.

But these students are not solely motivated by transactional achievement, in which doing something results in a tangible result. Achievement can also include advancement in learning. For example, helping students see the "big idea" of what the class is about can give them a vision for the course itself. Tying each activity and assignment back to the big idea may help students see that they are advancing to a greater level of knowledge and not solely accumulating points for a grade. Doing so might also help contribute to the applied nature of learning that Generation Z students enjoy.[70] And asking students what each assignment and activity has to do with the larger goal of the course can engage them in the conversation.

Knowing that the big idea is valuable to their future[71] and that all the steps along the way will help them get there may contribute to Generation Z's achievement motivation. So take the time to explain the real-life application of each learning activity and assignment, articulating that learning the subject matter will prepare them for the future as they advance through their careers.

FEELING STRESSED

In addition to their characteristics and motivations, it is important to understand circumstances that may influence learning. For one, Generation Z students are overwhelmingly stressed. Sixty-four percent of college seniors say they feel stressed out at least once a week.[72] In addition, 95 percent reported frequently or occasionally feeling overwhelmed by all they had to do.[73] Thus, Generation Z students may bring this stress to the classroom and their studies overall and would likely benefit from opportunities to manage that stress.

STRESS MANAGEMENT

Infusing stress management techniques in the curriculum can be critical to a student's educational experience. This was evident in the rationale for creating the SMART Lab at Ohio State University, which is designed to help students manage their stress before they are in crisis.[74] The lab offers both web-based programs and on-site volunteers to help with stress reduction, and students can take part in individual bio-feedback sessions or join a meditation group.[75] Other creative initiatives include George Mason University's digital badge on resilience students can earn by completing a 5-week work-shop[76] and the University of South Florida's MWell4Success plan that incorporates several campus-wide services and programs including a wellness center with stations for relaxation, wellness coaching, and required mental health literacy training for all students.[77] While not all institutions have the ability to create a facility or campus-wide initiative designed for stress management, strategies such as helping students engage in positive thinking[78] or employ time management techniques[79] have been associated with stress management and can be incorporated on a smaller scale into individual classes.

SUMMARY

Generation Z, like all generational cohorts, is marked by unique characteristics and strengths, motivations, and circumstances that impact their learning. It is important to keep in mind that understanding the nuances of Generation Z learners is critical to designing appropriate and effective experiences that maximize their learning.

4

THE INSTRUCTORS

Just as the learner is paramount to the learning environment, so too is the instructor. And while the expert at the front of the classroom imparting wisdom on students may be the stereotypical image of the quintessential educator, Generation Z has their own notions of what makes an exemplary instructor.

In both of our studies with Generation Z college students, we explored their perspectives, styles, and preferences related to learning. In our *Generation Z Goes to College* study, we asked students to describe their ideal learning environments, and in our *Generation Z Stories* study, we asked students to describe what makes learning enjoyable. Themes that emerged include specific instructor characteristics and behaviors; how they want to communicate, connect, and interact with their instructors; and their desire to not let the instructor down.

Characteristics and Behaviors

Generation Z students value specific characteristics and behaviors in their instructors. These center on being engaging and enthusiastic, having passion, demonstrating humor and wit, and being knowledgeable and experienced. In addition, with a generation that prefers an overwhelming amount of clarity in their learning process,[80,81] instructors who are able to provide some level of ambiguity and discuss the importance of this with their students may foster deeper learning.

Being Engaging and Enthusiastic

Generation Z students want their instructors to be engaging and enthusiastic.[82] A student in our *Generation Z Stories* study pointed out that learning is enjoyable "when the professor is engaging with the students, [is] easy to approach, [is] enthusiastic when teaching, and has a sense of humor."[83] If the instructor is not excited about the content, how can the students be? It is important to differentiate engaging instructional design from an engaging instructor. Having a dynamic activity does not make up for having an instructor who looks like they are bored or uninterested in the content. While we know that many instructors teach the same classes and same lesson plans multiple times and over many years, this generational cohort wants to feel the energy as if this information was being delivered with the zeal of the very first time.

Having Passion

Similarly, Generation Z students want their instructors to be passionate about their subject areas.[84] This goes beyond engaging students; they also want their instructors to exhibit an aura of love for the content, such as a math professor getting excited about statistics or an art teacher who is deeply moved when talking about specific art pieces. For Generation Z, this passion is contagious and can serve as a serious motivator for learning. One student pointed this out by saying, "Learning is most enjoyable when the person teaching me is passionate about the subject. Getting to see a person in their element, talking about something that gets them excited is what gets me excited to learn it."[85]

DEMONSTRATING HUMOR AND WIT

Generation Z is growing up in a time when there are memes, GIFs, funny videos on YouTube, and social media posts that offer them an opportunity for a good laugh. But they do not just want humor in their lives outside class; they want their instructors to insert a little humor and wit into the class.[86] Making a joke, even one not really that funny, shows students the instructor is making an effort to relax and let go of a serious tone for just a moment. One student pointed out the importance of humor by saying, "I personally like it when professors are witty and funny; it makes going to class enjoyable rather than just listening to a monotone lecture."[87] While it is important to not let humor and the notion of edutainment take over the learning environment so much that it distracts from the learning, it may be essential for a generation of students who crave transparency and authenticity[88] to see the less serious side of their instructors.

Possessing Knowledge and Experience

While it is important to Generation Z students that instructors are engaging and passionate about their fields as well as demonstrate a sense of humor, they also need to have both expertise and experience in the subject matter. Generation Z students want instructors who have studied the topic they are teaching, "have real-world experience," and perhaps even possess appropriate credentials.[89]

For example, Generation Z students want their instructors to have practical experience.[90] A music instructor who has never performed, a business instructor with no real-life business experience, or a computer programming instructor who has never programmed anything is not going to cut it with this generation. Their strong interest in applied learning[91] means they want to be taught by people who *have* applied the learning. And, as Generation Z students are concerned about how their learning applies to their future careers,[92] having instructors with practical experience (and likely networks in the field) can offer Generation Z students opportunities to receive guidance and mentorship.

Discussing the Difficulty of Learning

While Generation Z students overwhelmingly want their instructors to provide a great deal of description and clarity in regard to the learning process,[93] it is also important that students face some challenges in this process. When students experience confusion or disequilibrium in their learning, the emotion that emerges can actually increase the students' task engagement and ultimately result in their deeper-level understanding of the content.[94] So it may be important to discuss this with students, letting them know that ambiguity and uncertainty can be useful to their overall learning.

COMMUNICATION, CONNECTION, AND INTERACTION

Given that 11 percent of Generation Z students rank teachers as their number one role model, with another 42 percent ranking them as number two,[95] it is no surprise that many Generation Z students want to have meaningful connections with their instructors. One student said, "Being able to create a relationship with the professor makes learning enjoyable. When professors share their lives with you, it opens up an entire[ly] new point of view."[96]

FOSTERING CONNECTIONS

One activity that can help students and the instructor get to know each other involves incorporating a check-in at the beginning of class. This can be done on a regular basis or periodically. One method involves having each student share a low (a low point of the day or week) and a high (a high point or good news from that day or week). To create an equitable community, the instructor should share as well. If the class is quite large, have students share in groups of four with the instructor rotating between groups each class session.

Another idea is to incorporate technology into self-sharing. Each class session, have students be prepared to share a

GIF (an animated image) or a meme (an image or GIF reflective of a shared cultural situation, such as a funny snippet from a movie) of how their week has been going.[97] They can either share online using a class hashtag or they can send it to the instructor to post on a rolling slide deck for students to see when they enter class.

COMMUNICATING FACE-TO-FACE

It may seem that with all the technology available today that students would rather text than connect in person with others. In our *Generation Z Goes to College* study, though, we found that while they like texting, more prefer face-to-face communication.[98] How do we reconcile this phenomenon with the continued emergence of online and hybrid courses, virtual office hours (especially in higher education), and group projects that use digital platforms rather than in-person meetings? It seems as if there is simply a more digitized learning culture today. And while this generation craves human connection,[99] many think they lack necessary interpersonal skills to actually navigate these connections.[100] Some still want to talk to their instructors face-to-face rather than send a message. And if doing so in real life (IRL) is not always possible, video chat programs like Zoom, Google Hangouts, Skype, or even the institution's learning management system can offer a way to foster a connection with students similar to that of being face-to-face.

TEXTING

It is not surprising, given how much we see young people staring at their phones, that this generation likes to text.[101]

Instructors may not want to text message with their students because they do not want to share their personal cell phone number. However, texting may be the key to communicating with them.

For those who want one-way communication, platforms like Remind allow instructors to send text messages to students without them being able to text back or have access to their personal phone number. In addition, being able to preprogram all the reminder texts for the semester or year can ensure that students receive timely texts without instructors even having to remember to send them.

For those who want to give out their numbers so students can text them directly, another option is to get a free Google Voice number that can be forwarded to a personal number. For example, students can text or call the Google Voice number, and the instructor can respond without ever having to share their personal number with students.

EMAILING

While face-to-face communication and texting are preferred, very few Generation Z students like to use email.[102] This may not be surprising for many instructors given that comments such as, "I don't really check my email" or "I haven't checked my email since the beginning of the semester," seem to be everyday phrases for this generation. Yet why do instructors put so much time and effort into emailing very detailed, lengthy messages? Is it for the few students who may read these emails or to make sure there is some kind of account-ability paper trail that the information was shared? From what we know about Generation Z, if we really want them to have information, sending it over email should be only one of many communication options.

The issue with email and this generation is not just that many do not check their emails consistently or do not read them entirely or at all, some may lack the actual skill and demeanor required for writing a professional email. It makes sense that Generation Z students, who have a preference for other communication formats over email,[103] simply may have never been taught how to appropriately compose a message or engage in email communication etiquette. It is more than just the grammatical and formatting boost that students may need in order to send professional emails. Students need to keep in mind other elements such as timing and tone as well as how formal language in an email is different from that of informal social media messaging. Given that many may need to send emails more regularly in their future workplaces, it might be worth the time and investment to help them develop their capacities for drafting emails while in school. Students can also refer to the book, *Wait, How Do I Write This Email?*, for information about and templates for writing nearly any professional email.[104]

Another tool that may be useful in helping students send professional emails is to set email expectations. Requiring students to send appropriate and professional emails can help prepare them for their future experience in the workplace as well as make life a bit easier for the instructor who is on the receiving end of the email. For example, an email expectations policy can include content about general email netiquette, grammar tips, how to develop a signature line, and how to forward emails to accounts that are more often checked so as not to miss important messages. In addition, the following process outlined below can help students craft a professional and appropriate email to the course instructor.

Email Expectations Policy
Subject Line:

- Your email must have a subject line that includes the name of the course.

Greeting:

- Your email must have a greeting.
- <u>Examples:</u> "Hi Dr. ...," or "Dear Mr. ...," or "Hello Ms. ...,"
- Please do not just write "Dr. ....," or other title and name only. Always include a greeting. And absolutely don't just start writing the body of the email without the greeting, title, and name. A nice beginning sets the tone for a happy recipient.

Introduction:

- If emailing for the first time about a specific topic, make sure to introduce the context of who you are.

- <u>Example:</u> "My name is Ethan Peterson, and I'm in your ... class on Wednesdays."

Body–Part I:

- The first part of the body of the email should include either a question or information that you want to share (or both sometimes).
- <u>Example of a Question:</u> "What library databases would you recommend I use to search for information on ...?"
- <u>Example of Information Sharing:</u> "I wanted to reach out to let you know that I won't be in class next week. I plan to submit all assignments by the due date and will review the slides posted on the course website. I just thought I would give you a heads-up for class planning purposes."

Body–Part II:

- The second part of the body of the email (if asking a question) should include a description of everything you have done to answer this question on your own.
- <u>Examples:</u> "I have looked through the syllabus and on the course website and wasn't able to find out..." or "I have asked two classmates and wasn't able to track down..."

Salutation:

- Always end your emails with a closing like "Thank you," "Respectfully," or "Sincerely."
- Below that, include your signature line (with your full name).

Helping students develop email communication skills not only benefits the learners and the instructors to ensure all parties are on the same page but also assists Generation Z learners in developing important professional skills for their future careers.

STUDENTS NOT WANTING TO DISAPPOINT

Many in this generation are motivated by not wanting to let others down.[105] What this may mean for instructors is that students may want to perform or behave in appropriate ways not because they want to succeed but because they do not want to disappoint their instructors with whom they feel a connection. For example, a Generation Z student might approach an instructor and apologize for not having an assignment. Rather than asking for an extension (or perhaps in addition to), the student may apologize for letting the instructor down, saying "I don't want you to think poorly of me as a student." But this is not exactly the intrinsic motivation instructors might want students to have in regard to their interest and efforts for learning.[106] And it might also foster a need for external accolades from the instructor that leaves the student's desire for success on the shoulders of a relationship or perceived relationship with the instructor.

BUILDING AUTHENTIC RELATIONSHIPS

As there is inherently a power dynamic between instructor and student, and students may simply aim to please, it is important not to play into that dynamic as a way to get students to perform. Many Generation Z students are very concerned with what others think about them.[107] So it is important for instructors to consider authenticity and transparency with students as a whole so students can see that people make mistakes or are not always successful, even if they try really hard. This may make instructors more human to students so they can calibrate the extent of energy they put into pleasing their role model and instead put it into seeking guidance and feedback from an elder who might be able to help them learn and grow from mistakes.

FUELING INTRINSIC MOTIVATION

While it is important to foster a connection with students, finding a way to shift students' motivation from one of pleasing the instructor to one that draws from internal motivation can be critical for them to sustain the performance they want beyond the time they are in any particular class.[108] Perhaps at the beginning of the course, ask them to write down what motivates them to do well in school. Then have them discuss with a partner, spending more time on reasons that are associated with intrinsic motivation (e.g., wanting to do well for personal achievement, seeing evidence of their growth and learning, etc.). Ask students to discuss how they can tap into those more frequently to motivate themselves as they move through the course.

Summary

Generation Z students see their instructors as important people in their lives. In particular, these students feel that instructors with certain characteristics and behaviors and who get to know them personally are the most effective and most enjoyable to learn from. While instructors should find ways to connect with their Generation Z students, they also need to hold them to certain expectations around professional communication to both enhance the student-instructor interaction as well as prepare them for corresponding in a career or professional setting. And finding ways to foster their intrinsic motivation, rather than focusing on not letting the instructor down, may have a more lasting impact on their learning as they navigate their educational journey.

5

The Learning Environment

Thinking back fifty years ago, it was not uncommon to see classrooms set up with chairs and desks in rows facing the front of the room, with a good view of the chalkboard. Classroom technology included projectors for film strips and, later, overhead transparencies. In addition, without the internet, the library was the only place for accessing books and journals, and the microfiche room was where old newspaper articles were stored.

Today's modern classrooms have moveable seating, digital projectors, SMART boards, and wireless network connectivity. And libraries are more than just repositories for printed or archived publications. They are information centers where students have access to the internet, collaborative workspaces, and tinkering labs and can use computers populated with software critical for their academic programs. And while there, they can lounge in comfortable and modern seating and perhaps even have a coffee. These modern learning environments have emerged both out of technological innovation, making it possible to incorporate more digital learning tools into learning spaces, and a desire of educators to create more opportunities for engagement and interaction in regard to learning.[109]

While technological advancements in learning spaces may offer benefits for students, there are other elements of the environment that can contribute to Generation Z student learning. These include both the design of physical learning environments and the management of boundaries with personal devices in those spaces.

QUIET SETTING

Generation Z students have specific preferences regarding their learning environments, whether those are classrooms, libraries, or study spaces. Above all, the learning spaces need to be quiet.[110] Many of these students do not want to hear a lot of chatter while they are studying. One Generation Z student noted, "My ideal learning environment is a quiet place where I can hear myself think."[111] Likewise, they also want their learning environments to be free from distractions and allow them to focus.[112]

SOOTHING SOUNDS OR NONE AT ALL

Interestingly, many in Generation Z study and even attend class wearing earbuds or headphones. One student said that the ideal learning environment is "anywhere I can use my headphones."[113] This may seem contradictory to the notion of the quiet they want, yet piping in sound to mask out external noise is their version of quiet. For example, the app, Noisli, offers the opportunity to play any kind of sound to "improve focus and boost… productivity."[114] Not only can sounds of nature be played but also white noise to drown out any external sounds. One Generation Z student said, "I usually do best when I have white noise."[115]

Some in Generation Z, though, do not just listen to birds chirping or white noise through their earbuds; they play their favorite tunes.[116] Although listening to music while studying can have a positive effect on mood,[117] it can also cause negative interference with cognitive tasks.[118] For example, listening to music and reading can involve "overlapping cognitive processes" as both are auditory activities.[119] In addition, loud and fast music or music that is familiar to the student can be the most problematic in interfering with reading comprehension.[120] Given this research, perhaps the best course of action is to ask students to remove their earbuds when engaging in learning activities, especially if they are listening to music. And while some Generation Z students may simply want to have their earbuds in with nothing playing, doing so during class may be distracting to other students as well as the instructor.

IDEAL LEARNING SPACES

In addition to quiet, we found that Generation Z students prefer learning spaces that are clean, neat, and organized; have comfortable furniture (but not too comfortable so they can stay awake); are spacious enough for their items (including food and drink); and allow them the freedom to move around.[121] They also want these spaces to have good lighting, be outside or have a view of the outdoors, have access to fresh air, and maintain a comfortable temperature.[122] One Generation Z student sums the ideal space as "somewhere where I can feel calm enough to study."

CREATING AN IDEAL LEARNING ENVIRONMENT

One of the easiest ways to align with the preferences of Generation Z students is to integrate elements of their ideal learning environment into the classroom. For example, the following checklist may help in designing that ideal space.

- ***Clean, organize, and neaten the space.*** Having too much clutter or items in disarray can be distracting to Generation Z students when trying to learn.[123] Put things back where they belong, and if there is not enough storage, get some bins, boxes, or drawers to keep everything organized.
- ***Provide comfortable furniture.*** While this may not be in the purview of instructors to obtain class-room furniture, it is important to note that if given the option to select a classroom, picking one with comfortable furniture over another would likely be a good investment.
- ***Set up a spacious layout.*** Move the furniture so that students feel they have enough personal space as well as enough space for them to freely move around the classroom.

- ***Have good lighting.*** This may mean turning all the lights on (even though sometimes it is tempting to leave one switch off if there are multiple) and even acquiring a lamp or two for both making the room lighter and creating a homey feel.
- ***Open a window.*** Students want both a view of the outside and fresh air. If there is a window in the classroom that can be opened, as long as weather permits, keep it open for that fresh breeze.
- ***Allow food and drink.*** While it may be the norm for many students to bring coffee or snacks into class (especially in college), it might be a nice offering for the instructor to bring in cookies or treats for the class periodically. And while not all classrooms allow food and drink, giving a snack break for a few minutes would be a nice touch.
- ***Watch the temperature.*** It can be easy to get distracted when one is too hot or too cold. So keeping the temperature of the room at a reasonable level could contribute to both engagement and learning. Although some classrooms are automatically climate controlled, it may prove useful to ask maintenance for an adjustment if the temperature is too extreme one way or the other or to request a different classroom, if possible.

TAKING IT OUTSIDE

Many Generation Z students enjoy learning outside.[124] One said, "I love how the outdoors relaxes me enough to concentrate on what I have to do."[125] While not always possible, just moving class or a class activity outside periodically might be rejuvenating for students. But be aware that this generation ranks naturalistic learning, which involves being "in touch with nature" and "studying natural phenomenon in a natural setting,"[126] very low on their list of preferences.[127] This means they want to sit outside but not want to incorporate the outdoors into the curriculum.

FINDING COMFORTABLE CAMPUS NOOKS

Whether it is an area by the stacks on the second floor of the library or a bench near a big tree on the outskirts of campus, many places offer Generation Z students an ideal learning environment. If there are self-directed tasks during class, give students a set time period and let them know that they can go within a particular radius of the classroom to find an ideal spot where they can work on the task before returning to class. While there might be a few minutes of transit time each way and some students may get off task, if the students are accountable to a deliverable when they get back to class, they may find a way to naturally calibrate their energy to get the task done.

HELPING STUDENTS DEVELOP HEALTHY BOUNDARIES WITH DEVICES

As many in this generation are not just tech-savvy but also tech-dependent, it is no surprise that Generation Z students would want to have access to and use their personal digital devices, such as phones, during class. Research has found that 70 percent of students say the biggest advantage to using their devices during class is so they can stay connected to others.[128] The concept of FOMO (the *fear of missing out* as discussed earlier) may help explain why some in Generation Z check their phones incessantly.[129] Researchers found that college students, in particular, who scored high on a FOMO scale had a stronger need to check their social media accounts while in class compared to students with lower FOMO scores.[130]

In addition, 60 percent of college students say they use their devices because they are bored in class.[131] In specifically looking at Generation Z, the data can be telling. While both Generation Z students and their older counterparts most frequently use their devices during class to look up course information and send messages, Generation Z students, more specifically, engage in online photo sharing during class at a far higher rate than older students.[132] In our research, we found that Instagram is where Generation Z students go to share about themselves, and Snapchat is where they connect with their friends.[133] Given that apps such as these came of age along with Generation Z, it is no surprise that younger students who grew up with online photo sharing sites have high usage rates.

In addition to reaching out to the external world during class through their personal devices, some Generation Z students are messaging each other right in class using their laptops. A new trend is for students to either open a document on Google Docs to "take notes" or copy a document shared by the instructor, creating a similar page name for the new document. Once the document is open, students can then invite their friends to edit it, allowing them to covertly write notes to each other in a group chat[134] without having to use their phones, which can be easily discernable for instructors, or a messaging platform on their computers that can be seen on the screen from afar.

While they may be messaging or on photo sharing sites during class, many Generation Z students refrain from engaging in doing anything online that requires a great deal of cognitive energy. For example, very few are surfing the web, reading news feeds, watching videos, listening to music, and playing video games during class.[135] Thus, it appears that their interactions with their devices are reserved for quick transactional tasks. Regardless if their learning is interrupted only by short moments of engagement with their devices, the presence of these devices in the classroom at all can have a negative effect on learning.[136] There are, however, several approaches to addressing this issue with Generation Z students.

SETTING EXPECTATIONS

One strategy to address the use of personal digital devices during class is to set clear expectations with students. Whether instituting a no-device policy[137] or a modified one that may include using technology only during breaks, it is important that instructors make sure students understand the rationale for the policy in terms of how it aligns with the course.[138]

In addition, it is imperative that instructors enforce the policy,[139] or it may carry no weight with the students.

Also, getting students involved in holding themselves accountable for their tech use during class may have some advantages. Consider having students create classroom standards that address the use of personal devices in the classroom.[140] That way, they all agree to the parameters for use and can hold each other accountable to their own expectations.

SHARING RESEARCH ON DIGITAL DISTRACTIONS

Members of Generation Z often engage in multitasking.[141] They may text on their phones, post photos on social media, surf the web, stream a video, and listen to music through their earbuds at the same time—all while trying to learn. And although this may seem exhausting to think about, this generation does not get overwhelmed in doing all of these tasks at once. Those in Generation Z believe they are good at multitasking and that doing so does not compromise the quality of their work.[142] However, many Generation Z students are concerned about not doing their best[143] and not completing a task accurately.[144] So perhaps letting them know that studies have found that using their devices during class for non-course-related tasks may prevent them from doing their best or accurately completing tasks, which could, in turn, negatively affect their grades.[145]

OFFERING ENGAGING INSTRUCTION

With Generation Z students indicating that one of the main reasons they use their devices during class is boredom,[146] instructors must take note. For example, lecturing directly from slides or the textbook might not just be boring; it might be a duplication for students if they have access to those resources outside class and can refer to them on their own. Students may be thinking, "Why pay attention when I can read this later?" or "I already read this for homework; now I just have to sit here bored while the instructor repeats the same information."

This does not mean that every minute of instruction needs to be as entertaining as a silly online video, but it is a call for engaging students. Presenting new content in class that cannot be accessed in a print or digital resource might not just make the class more engaging but also increase attendance (specifically in college courses) as the material would not be available anywhere but in class. So, if a student disengages during class to use their device, they would likely miss critical information they cannot get anywhere else.

In addition, consider incorporating different hands-on and applied activities during class. These types of activities resonate with Generation Z students[147] and might be so engaging that they stay off their personal devices.

HELPING STUDENTS MANAGE BOUNDARIES WITH PERSONAL DEVICES

Another idea to help students create healthy boundaries with their devices is to integrate tech breaks into class. This involves giving students periodic one-minute breaks to get on their devices, making sure to extend the time between breaks each week so there are fewer breaks over time.[148] Giving them breaks allows those with high levels of FOMO to perhaps not feel so disconnected or off the grid for an extended period, reducing their anxiety or urge to check their devices because they know that there is a specified time to do so. Another idea is to have students mute their notifications but keep their devices nearby. Doing so may result in less anxiety for them than putting their devices away and out of sight.[149]

INCORPORATING PERSONAL DEVICES IN CLASS

Another approach to dealing with the proliferation of personal devices in the classroom is simply to incorporate them into the learning environment. For example, it was not too long ago when a trip to the school or campus library during class was commonplace. But today, students can look up information online without a library visit. Consider giving them time during class to work on an upcoming assignment and letting them use their devices for research or writing.

In addition, because Generation Z students enjoy image-based platforms[150] and streaming videos,[151] having them use educational apps, take pictures, or make videos during class may engage them in learning or developing content while allowing them to be on their devices.

SUMMARY

For Generation Z, the environment plays a significant role in their learning. Many in this generation want a quiet place to learn that feels natural, open, comfortable, and like home. And while they may want to multitask on their devices in these learning environments, it is important that instructors help students create healthy boundaries with their digital devices—both for their academic success and their engagement in the course material.

6

INSTRUCTIONAL DESIGN

Each new generation brings a unique set of values, preferences, styles, and motivations to the learning environment. But just knowing more about today's Generation Z learners is not enough. It is critical to design learning experiences that align with their preferences for intrapersonal, social, experiential, demonstrated, and digital learning.

INTRAPERSONAL LEARNING

One of the most preferred learning methods for Generation Z students is intrapersonal learning,[152] which involves "engaging in independent projects."[153] and incorporates self-direction, self-pacing, self-reflection, and self-reliance. But not all attributes of intrapersonal learning resonate with Generation Z. For example, we found in both of our studies that they need a lot of structure and guidance in their learning.[154,155] One Generation Z student reflects this by saying,

"I like to know exactly what to do."[156] Thus, self-directed learning would not seem to align with their preference for structure unless they had limited choices from which to direct their learning.

On the other hand, this is a generation that likes self-paced learning[157] in the sense that they want to decide how they want to spend their time—perhaps going deeper into investigating subject matter that is of interest to them or studying topic X before topic Y. But in terms of deciding deadlines, Generation Z students want those clearly laid out before them.[158] Having deadlines for assignments (not just due dates but also "you may want to have completed this part by…" indicators) aligns with their desire for a sense of structure.[159] One student highlights this by saying, "I am a person who likes structure and scheduling."[160]

In today's social media age where likes and comments are a daily reminder of one's apparent self-worth, it is not surprising that many Generation Z students are fearful of being judged by their peers or instructors for saying the wrong answer.[161] This hesitance or second-guessing does not seem to align with the practice of self-reflection where there might not be a correct answer. One Generation Z student said, "I do not like self-reflection and open-endedness and group discussions."[162] Their learning process is often more like a quest to get the one correct answer and not an opportunity to grapple with multiple interpretations, especially if they believe those interpretations may be judged by their peers. This theme rippled through our research.[163] For example, one student said an ideal learning environment is one where "I would be able to ask questions without fear of judgment and without having to speak up in front of a large group."[164]

However, this is a generation that wants to learn by themselves and be accountable for their own academic performance. One Generation Z student comments on this by saying, "I prefer to learn independently, involving others only when I must."[165] This is understandable given that they identify as self-reliant, determined, and responsible.[166] They like to learn independently and be responsible for doing assignments on their own. One student said an ideal learning environment is one where "I'm not required to do a lot of group papers."[167] Even those who appeared to be open to group work had boundaries in that an ideal environment is one "where people actually pull their own weight in group projects."[168] Their preference for intrapersonal learning coupled with their self-reliance and determination may influence their desire to work alone as opposed to working in groups.

STRUCTURING CHOICE

Given that many in Generation Z prefer structure and clear guidelines,[169,170] there is value in providing a sense of choice, especially as they engage in intrapersonal learning where decisions are their own. Perhaps it might be too limitless to ask students to find a reading about a topic and bring it to class, especially given the vast amount of information available online today. But they could choose from approved readings that had been selected by the instructor. Being able to select a reading among many choices, for example, might foster a sense of independence with this generation while assuring them that ANY of the choices would be acceptable. And when students are interested in something (like the reading they selected), they tend to be more motivated to engage in behaviors related to that interest (like actually reading what they selected).[171]

The notion of choice also applies to assignments, in that students could choose from a selection of different, yet equally rigorous, assignments to complete. For example, students could write a five-page paper, record a ten-minute video, or do a fifteen-minute presentation, all with the goal of students learning about specific subject matter.

PACING THE LEARNING

Because Generation Z students are motivated by milestones,[172] it is critical to set a variety of deadlines so they can see those milestones laid out before them. But it may be that the only milestone for completing a large assignment is the assignment due date itself, as instructors hope that students will not wait until just before an assignment is due to start working on it. Procrastination, however, is not a phenomenon discovered by this generation of young people, nor will it end with this generation. Knowing that some may not necessarily create their own milestones and are also not accountable to their peers if they are engaging in intrapersonal learning, it might be important to have smaller projects due throughout the course that culminate into one large end-of-semester assignment.

These small projects essentially integrate pacing into the course schedule, requiring students to be working toward the larger project throughout the duration of the course, even in smaller chunks.

OFFERING SPACE FOR MULTIPLE INTERPRETATION

The notion that there may be multiple ways to interpret content can be uncomfortable for many in Generation Z. One Generation Z student noted that an ideal learning environment is one where "teachers actually answer questions, not dance around them."[173] Another said, "I like to be able to ask questions and have [them] be answered clearly."[174]

Their desire for detailed instructions and concrete answers likely trumps their openness to derive their own meaning, which can be a hallmark for the self-reflective nature of intrapersonal learning. While Generation Z students describe themselves as having high levels of perspective taking,[175] which involves considering multiple perspectives from others, they appear to struggle with deriving their own when there is no clear-cut answer. This does not mean that instructors should shy away from creating a learning environment that fosters some cognitive dissonance. It just means that some in this generation may need more opportunities to come up with their own unique perspective.

FLIPPING THE LEARNING

Much attention has been paid to the notion of flipped learning, which involves engaging in pre-learning experiences before class. This model may be a good fit for Generation Z students for a number of reasons. First, their desire for intrapersonal learning makes it easy to assign homework ahead of time that they do on their own to prepare for class. Second, they have access to so much information that they can learn what they need prior to class with the right resources. And third, with many in this generation having a fear of emotional distress,[176] trying to learn and participate in class at the same time may be overwhelming. It may be useful to create a multitude of pre-learning experiences before class to help prepare students. Then, when they come to class, they are ready to engage in the application of the material.

For students to actually do pre-learning, a few things need to take place. First, there must be quality opportunities for pre-learning that align with how Generation Z prefers to learn. For example, because video-based learning is an effective learning method for them,[177] consider assigning videos, TED Talks, and online tutorials in lieu of or in addition to course readings. These mediums provide Generation Z students the opportunity to re-watch the pre-learning content as many times as they would like until they feel they are prepared for class.

Second, while it would be ideal for students to do the required readings or watch the required videos because of their inherent desire to learn, the reality is that unless there is some accountability measure in place, some will likely not complete the pre-class work. Consider having a short application paper or a reflection that they complete before class or an in-class application assignment, synthesis paper, or journal response to a big question to start each class. Even Generation Z students themselves believe that these types of accountability measures would motivate them to complete their assigned readings, in particular.[178]

BUILDING CONFIDENCE

Generation Z students' desire for intrapersonal learning may also be related to a lack of confidence or desire to take a risk.[179] For some in Generation Z, being asked to share the right answer in front of the entire class elicits a fear of being judged by their peers and the instructor if they are incorrect.[180] Allowing time for students to research or reflect on their own before being asked to share in front of others could build up their confidence. It might not be that they do not know the answer but instead just need a few moments to prepare their thoughts before participating. One Generation Z student discussed this apprehension by saying, "I like to think everything through first and organize my thoughts and present when I know I am on the right track."[181]

More specifically, to engage everyone in the class, give students a set amount of time to research a topic, after which they would complete a short writing reflection. Once everyone has had a chance to research and reflect, ask students to share their reflections with the entire class. Doing so would require participation from all students and not just the vocal ones who would have participated regardless.

Further, it may be that to build confidence, students need to experience times where they do not know the answer or give an incorrect one in front of others. Then it might not seem as daunting or frightening to at least offer a response without a guarantee that it is correct. To set the tone for students to take risks in class, it might be useful to set class standards around the importance of inquiry and the value of offering ideas, even if they might be incorrect.

Another way to address students' fear of not knowing or giving a wrong answer involves having everyone, including the instructor, share a time when they thought they knew something but actually did not. To do this, everyone shares what they thought they knew, what the correct answer was, and what the experience of being incorrect was like. This sharing exercise may help break down barriers between students and the instructor by demonstrating that no one in the room is always right, even the instructor.

TEACHING ONE-ON-ONE

Many Generation Z students crave one-on-one connection with their instructors, both from a relationship standpoint[182] and from a need for clarity in completing their assignments and ensuring their learning is on track.[183] One student described the ideal learning environment as "me and the teacher."[184]

This individualized learning also stems from their interest in learning content that is facilitated rather than presented.[185] In an ideal environment, the classroom would become a learning lab where students work individually and the instructor roams the room checking in periodically and offering one-on-one customized help as needed.[186] One student noted this preference by saying that an ideal learning environment involves working "1 on 1 with the teacher/professor, being able to ask as many questions as needed, and get[ting] hands[-]on help from them as the need arises."[187] Our studies show that if they had it their way, many would opt to take a class in which they were the only student.[188]

Knowing it is not really possible to have a class of one, taking a cue from that preference, however, could point to engaging in more one-on-one student time during and outside class. For example, provide a self-directed learning task during class and then rotate between students to check in on their progress or even hold required meetings with each student outside of class to check in on progress. Or, with smaller classes, institute individualized learning by converting one or two class sessions into blocked one-on-one required appointments with the instructor and student. Each student would have a set amount of uninterrupted time with the instructor to ask questions, get feedback, clarify assignments, or just forge a relationship.

SOCIAL LEARNING

An interesting characteristic of Generation Z is that although they prefer intrapersonal learning, they do not necessarily want to learn by themselves. They are, in essence, social learners.[189] At first glance, these preferences appear to be contradictory as social learning insinuates some type of group or interpersonal learning, which many of these students do not enjoy.[190] Although they do not want to learn with others, they want to learn next to them. A Generation Z study group might look like several students gathered together, all with earbuds in, studying on their own. They likely made a conscious effort to be in the same space at the same time to study but have no interest in actively engaging with the group while they study. How then can instructors balance the desire for intrapersonal and social learning with this generation?

HYBRID OVER ONLINE COURSES

Generation Z students' desire for intrapersonal learning appears to align well with online courses. They could work at their own pace, study when they want, and if the course is asynchronous, not attend class at all. This would be the ultimate self-learning experience. However, an entirely online course, especially one that is asynchronous, would not feed Generation Z's need for social learning.[191] It is not surprising then that only 13 percent of those in Generation Z would choose an online course over a class that meets in person.[192] It is important for many in this generation to have some periodic opportunities for face-to-face connection with the instructor and other students. This may mean having synchronous sessions of an online course or, even better, offering the course as a hybrid with a combination of self-learning and intermittent in-person sessions with the larger class. To integrate a flipped approach, students would first engage in self-directed learning around specific content followed by face-to-face sessions where they practice and apply that content.

PEER SUPPORT AND ASSISTANCE

Another element of social learning that resonates with Generation Z is their desire to learn around others who are smart, motivated, and driven to succeed. They like "smart and engaged learners,"[193] and want to study and learn in "a room full of genius people."[194] While they want to focus on their own learning, some want others around who they "can bounce ideas off."[195] Because of this, it may be helpful to encourage students to informally—or even more so, formally—put together or join a study group even if there is little interaction between the students when they come together. Just being around others who are motivated and engaged could help students focus on their own learning while having others to consult with if they have a question or thought.

EXPERIENTIAL LEARNING

Many Generation Z students also prefer experiential learning.[196] They like to engage in hands-on experiences that allow them to situate themselves in the middle of the learning rather than on the periphery as an observer. This means applying the content they have learned to develop ideas, create innovations, and solve problems. Research has found that both sixth through twelfth graders and their teachers believe students learn best by doing or creating.[197] And this desire for experiential learning is not just prevalent in K–12; it was also an emergent theme in our study at the college level.[198] One Generation Z college student said, "I need to be actively doing the learning to obtain the most information."[199]

INTERACTIVE ACTIVITIES

Given the myriad of teaching activities available online and in publications, instructors have many resources to choose from for integrating experiential learning. And while it might not be surprising that Generation Z students have a strong interest in experiential learning as interactive activities can be fun and engaging, it is validating to know that continuing to integrate experiential learning into the curriculum works well for the vast majority of students in this generation.[200]

PEER LEARNING

Peer learning, which involves one student teaching one or more peers, has many benefits for all students involved. But for the students who are teaching, the experience can help them better learn the material, develop their organizational skills, and practice providing feedback to others.[201] These students can also experience the material in ways that are not limited to being the receiver of knowledge but instead the facilitator of it for others. During peer learning, students can create curriculum and develop innovative activities. They may even need to tap into their problem-solving skills to make adjustments in the moment if the learning is not occurring as planned.

DEMONSTRATED LEARNING

Many Generation Z students also have a desire for learning opportunities where they learn how to do something and then practice and get feedback.[202] One Generation Z student sums this up by saying, "Show me something. Tell me how it works, why it works, things that work similarly. Let me do it, show me how to improve it. Let me think about it for an [hour or day]. Show me again; let me practice again."[203]

DEMONSTRATIONS

One method that instructors can use to help Generation Z students learn is to show them first what is expected of them. One student in our study described this by saying, "I like to see an experienced person do something first, then [have it] become a part of my own learning experience."[204] While this seems pretty standard in subjects such as math or science, using demonstrations of other less technical tasks (e.g. showcasing effective writing practices or demonstrating how to approach a case study) might help Generation Z students better engage in learning activities and complete course assignments. And it is not just about showing them each step in the process; Generation Z students want to know why they are doing each step. One Generation Z student noted the importance of "observing firsthand someone skilled performing the task while explaining why they do each step the way they do."[205]

Not all demonstrations need to be live during class either. Instructors can put together video tutorials or voiceover demonstrations on platforms such as Voice Thread, Jing, or Camtasia. Recording a demonstration allows instructors to script, prepare, and re-record the demonstration until it is exactly the way they want it, unlike a live demonstration during class. And with a recorded demonstration, students can view it as many times as they would like.

DIGITAL LEARNING

It is not surprising with the number of digital platforms available, both educational and mainstream, that many in this generation enjoy using technology. And although technology can be distracting in a learning environment if not purposely linked to learning, it can also offer many educational opportunities. We have to remember that many in Generation Z grew up with the Khan Academy and Google Classroom. They are used to using technology for learning, whether that is researching online, watching online tutorials and instructional videos, taking tests, or engaging in collaborative writing.

VIDEO-BASED LEARNING

Many Generation Z students prefer learning from videos on YouTube over text on Google.[206] So it may be helpful to weave into the curriculum videos from TED-Ed, The Open University on iTunes U, The Great Courses, or shows from educational channels on YouTube such as Crash Course or Big Think.

ENGAGING APPS AND PLATFORMS

There are also engaging digital apps and platforms that can be used during class, whether on a students' personal device or one already in the classroom. For example, polling apps like Kahoot.it or PollEverywhere allow students to vote on a phone, tablet, or computer with the aggregate results showing up on a master poll that the instructor can display for everyone to see. These apps can serve as an interactive way to engage students in learning new content as well as provide a means for a mid-class check-in to gauge learning progress.

Digital apps and platforms do not just offer a way for instructors to present material in an engaging manner during class but also provide students with alternatives to traditional paper and pencil learning assessment both during and outside class. For example, with iMovie, students can create their own tutorials, presentations, or even reports or book summaries.[207] And sites such as Swipe, an interactive presentation platform, and Explain Everything, a mobile whiteboard, offer creative ways for students to showcase their learning.

THE ROLE OF SOCIAL MEDIA IN LEARNING

Generation Z students spend a lot of time on social media and crave relationships with their instructors,[208] but that does not mean they want to "friend," "connect," or "link" with them. The creepy treehouse phenomenon, originally defined in a higher education context by Jared Stein from Utah Valley University, alludes to the notion that some social media platforms should be reserved only for young people, having no adult interference.[209] Some instructors, though, believe that connecting with students on social media can break down the student-teacher barrier and thus create the relationships that

Generation Z so craves.[210] For instructors who do "friend" their current students, it is highly advisable to closely monitor personal social media platforms to make sure they are appropriate and professional for students to see as well as work directly with the institution to ensure compliance with any specific policies.

Regardless if instructors and students connect on social media, it is important to remember that not all students will want to use social media platforms for school work. So, before requiring students to join a class group on a social media platform or use a particular social media account to complete an assignment, consider other uses of social media that can be effective in a learning environment. For one, perhaps encourage students to share social media handles with their peers so they can connect with each other to study or work on group projects. The students can create online groups, use video chat to meet, or message each other with information or questions. But it is on their terms and with their peers.

In addition, because hashtags can be used with nearly any social media platform,[211] create a class hashtag that students can use to post about course-related information if they are interested. The hashtag option, however, may require some monitoring to ensure that what is posted is educationally appropriate. Or find a hashtag already being used related to the course content. For example, if students are reading a book by particular author for class, perhaps there is already a hashtag where the students can jump in and read what others (even outside their class) post about that book.

Another idea is to use social media as the subject matter to be studied. For example, have students analyze content that others have posted on social media to better understand certain phenomena, like communication styles or political views.

Finally, consider using social media as a template for an assignment. Instead of having students post on their social media account for a class assignment, have them complete a persuasive essay in blog format, create a thesis statement for a paper using the format of Twitter that has a 240-character limit, or make their own memes about something they learned. While they are welcome to post any of this content online, it should be voluntary and not tied to assignment expectations.

SUMMARY

There are five main frameworks for learning approaches that resonate with Generation Z students—intrapersonal, social, experiential, demonstrated, and digital learning. Regardless of the course content, any or all of these may be infused into the course curriculum or assignments by using the pedagogical approaches associated with them.

7

CONTENT

While the subject of the course will need to be the main focus, spending some class time on content that aligns with preferences of Generation Z students can be beneficial. For example, weaving in topics such as emotional intelligence, success skills, life and career application, and social change can help students not only learn useful information but also do so in the context of a particular course subject.

EMOTIONAL INTELLIGENCE

Emotional intelligence involves "being aware that emotions can drive our behavior and impact people (positively or negatively), and learning how to manage those emotions—both our own and others—especially when we are under pressure."[212] But with Generation Z students' self-admitted low levels of interpersonal skills[213] and the fact that they spend a greater amount of time on social media than in person with their friends,[214] we have a cohort of students who would benefit from opportunities to develop their emotional intelligence skills. So, not only is it important for students to develop emotional intelligence skills for the workforce,[215] at the college level, in particular, those with higher levels of emotional intelligence tend to have higher levels of cognitive and affective engagement.[216]

INCORPORATING SOCIAL AND EMOTIONAL LEARNING IN K–12

Emotional intelligence is not a new phenomenon in the K–12 system as programs focusing on social and emotional learning are becoming more widespread.[217] These programs are often at the institution level and focus on a variety of competencies related to self and interpersonal awareness and management. The Collaborative to Advance Social and Emotional Learning created a framework of skills that includes "self-awareness, self-management, social awareness, relationship skills, and responsible decision-making and problem-solving."[218]

Due to money, resources, and time, it may not be feasible to offer school-wide programs aimed at developing students' social and emotional learning. But individual instructors can weave social and emotional lessons into the curriculum or frame existing activities in the context of social and emotional learning.

INFUSING EMOTIONAL INTELLIGENCE ACROSS THE COLLEGE CURRICULUM

At the college level, offering a standalone general education or even elective course in emotional intelligence could contribute significantly to student development and career preparation. But like K–12, it may not be feasible to launch a large initiative such as an entire course on emotional intelligence open to the whole student population. In that case, weaving elements of emotional intelligence into existing courses may be more realistic. There are many resources for both curriculum and assignments that can be used in a variety of courses across disciplines. For example, the *Emotionally Intelligent Leadership for Students: Facilitation and Activity Guide*[219] offers emotional intelligence curriculum designed specifically for students.

SUCCESS SKILLS

While it may seem that there are some critical skills that all students are expected to possess, this generation may be coming into our classrooms underprepared or needing development with those very skills. Consider that 24 percent of college seniors reported never having led a group toward achieving a common goal, and 15 percent said they did not know how to conduct research.[220] And given these are college seniors who have had years of college behind them, it is understandable to think that far more of those who are younger need experience and skill development in these areas.

Without these types of skills, it can be more challenging for students to learn course content. For example, assigning a group project for a history class might seem like a great way to offer an interactive and experiential learning experience for students to better understand history. But this approach rests on the notion that the students know how to effectively work in groups and that the group experience will not be a detriment or distraction to their learning about history.

ENHANCING SKILLS FOR ACADEMIC SUCCESS

One strategy to help enhance critical skills for engaging in learning involves instructors identifying skills students would need to effectively engage in a learning experience and then making time in the curriculum to provide instruction or resources for developing those skills. These skills may include working in groups, designing and giving a presentation, writing a paper using a particular format, researching information online, reading for deep comprehension, or synthesizing content into a short report. If students have the appropriate skill set to do the assignment, it may be that they are able to spend more time on the content and less on trying to navigate the medium around which the learning experience is designed.

LIFE AND CAREER APPLICATION

While many Generation Z students appreciate the process of learning and the general nature of knowledge acquisition,[221] they also want their educational experiences directly tied to their lives and future careers.[222] They want to make sure they are spending their time learning content where they see explicit real-life applicability, now and in the future.[223]

BRINGING IN REAL-LIFE SCENARIOS

Regardless of course content, Generation Z students need their learning experiences to be based on real life. For example, they enjoy subject matter that is connected to current events and issues.[224] So consider framing prompts for in-class discussions or developing assignments around the application of course content to a contemporary issue. Pulling modern-day events into the curriculum can help students understand their learning in the context of something larger while giving them a deeper understanding of a societal issue.

And real-world issues do not always have to be from the news. Generation Z students like to see how the content they are learning aligns with their personal experiences.[225] One way to help students make this connection is by integrating their experiences into the curriculum. For example, instead of providing a prewritten case scenario to students, have each student develop a scenario based on a real-life personal situation, similar to infusing family situations into case studies as discussed earlier. Then, select one for the whole class to address.

ENHANCING PROFESSIONAL SKILLS

In addition to critical thinking and creativity discussed earlier, the World Economic Forum identified three additional skills that will be necessary for future employees. These include complex problem-solving, people management, and coordinating with others.[226] In this sense, students need these skills regardless of their specific future career. And given that many in this generation want to learn new skills,[227] incorporating skill development into the curriculum would likely be welcomed.

One idea would be to ask each student to find a current or former professional in a career field related to the course who would be willing to talk with the class about developing critical skills for that profession. Reaching out to professionals to come to class would require students to research a related career field and engage in networking skills when extending the invitation.

HELPING THEM HELP OTHERS

Many Generation Z students want to use the information they learn to help others.[228] One student in our *Generation Z Stories* study said, "What makes learning enjoyable is being able to incorporate what I learn into my life and to make my life better for myself and for others around me."[229] To help them help others, instructors need to make explicit connections between learning and potential impact. One example involves letting future teachers know that enhancing their knowledge of assessment can help them better determine where their future students might need learning assistance. Another example involves sharing with future graphic designers the importance of being familiar with copyright laws to help their companies avoid copyright infringement.

SOCIAL CHANGE

Generation Z students are social change-minded, wanting to solve the world's problems rather than addressing the symptoms of those problems.[230] They are motivated by making a difference for others, and many feel that the desire to make an impact is fundamental to their professional calling.[231] One Generation Z student in our *Generation Z Stories* study said,

"If I can learn something that I can use to help another person, create something new, solve a problem, or expand my own self, I enjoy learning it."[232] And given that most are motivated by being able to advocate for something they believe in,[233] it makes sense that once that know what it is they believe in, they will be on a mission for social change.

HELPING THEM DISCOVER AND ARTICULATE THEIR PASSIONS

Making a difference is a bit elusive without understanding the passion behind that desired impact. While some students know early in their lives what their passions entail, others may not have a clue. Or at least they have not articulated their interests, values, and cares about the world in a sense that feels to them like a passion. To uncover a passion, it is important to help students identify what they care about. Any of the following three exercises can be used to stimulate their thinking:

- Have students create a vision statement for the world. "If the world was in its ideal state, it would look like…" (e.g. no pollution, fair treatment of everyone, etc.)
- Have students list five things they care about, other than their friends and family (e.g. animals, having healthy food to eat, getting a good job, etc.).
- Have students list three societal problems they wish were solved (e.g. amount of plastic produced, inequality, cost of college).

Once students have articulated some issues they care about, have them select one (perhaps the one that is most important to them, if they know) and think about how that issue might fit into their lives (career, personal, community, etc.). The following two exercises can help them uncover ways they can engage in making a difference around that issue:

- Have students research an organization working to make a difference around the issue they selected. Have them identify what role they would want to play within the organization to help address the issue.
- Have the students write a destiny statement—a statement of their calling to address their selected issue. For example, some students might describe loving to work individually with people, whereas others might enjoy investigating and solving problems. How could what they love to do help them address an issue they care about?

These exercises are broad enough to weave into a variety of types of courses and connect to the specific content related to the associated course subject.

FROM SERVICE LEARNING TO SOCIAL CHANGE LEARNING

Generation Z students want to engage in ways that involve fundamentally changing the structure of what is causing a social issue to persist rather than addressing the symptoms of the issue.[234] For example, they want to build a well where water is needed rather than deliver water jugs that would need to be refilled regularly. But service learning often involves engaging students in short-term service opportunities where their involvement aids with the symptoms of an issue (e.g. packaging food at a food pantry rather than addressing the underlying issue of hunger and poverty). While we know that engaging in service to addresses the symptoms of a larger issue is important, especially for those directly impacted by the issue, is there room in the curriculum for additional methods of service learning that tap into Generation Z's interest in social change?[235] For example, broadening the definition of service to include action research, entrepreneurship, and social innovation can offer ways for Generation Z students to make a difference in the lives of others in ways that align with their desire for social change.[236]

Action research, for one, involves "researching best practices, promising programs, or data to support policy initiatives."[237] The purpose is to come up with ideas that might help advance the thinking and strategy to solve a critical issue. One way for students to engage in action research is through a case competition. Students compete in teams, researching and presenting ideas to help solve a problem presented by a set of stakeholders. Arizona State University has their own event centered on action research, Change the World, during which students engage in pitch competitions to share their "best ideas and projects in education, sustainability, technology, and health."[238]

Another way to engage students in social change is through entrepreneurship. With large numbers of workers in the gig economy[239] and the desire for nearly half of those in Generation Z to work for themselves,[240] many Generation Z students will go on to be self-employed (if they are not already). While students who study business will have opportunities to learn about entrepreneurship, not many other students will. Incorporating entrepreneurship into the course curriculum (regardless of course subject) can offer both career preparation and a vehicle to engage in social change. For example, have students create a business plan for a mock organization dedicated to addressing a social issue they care about. This could be useful in any number of courses from writing to social sciences. Another idea is for the institution to provide mini-grants for a selected number of small student start-ups designed to work toward solving a societal problem. Students would fill out an institutional grant application and make their case as to how they plan to use the mini-grant to work toward social change. Not only do these strategies fit with Generation Z's interest in social change, but they also align with their desire for hands-on, practical learning.[241]

An additional method to help Generation Z students participate in social change involves incorporating opportunities to engage in social innovation. Nearly 40 percent of those in Generation Z plan to develop an invention.[242] This inventive spirit and innovative mindset can be leveraged to help them solve social issues. For example, hackathons are events where individuals or teams compete during a specified time frame in a common space to develop some type of useful technology around a particular idea.[243] Using this model, hosting a hackathon to develop an invention around a particular social issue would tap into the innovative capacities of some in Generation Z to make a difference.

SUMMARY

Regardless of course subject, Generation Z students would benefit from weaving certain content into the curriculum. For instance, spending time enhancing students' emotional intelligence and success skills can help prepare them for the future as well as maximize their learning while in school. In addition, focusing on life and career application, as well as social change, can help "bring the 'real world' into the classroom and the classroom into the 'real world.'"[244]

8

ASSIGNMENTS

An important factor to consider with Generation Z students is that a great deal of their learning happens outside the classroom. Thus, it is critical to ensure that assignments are developed to maximize their learning potential. There are five elements to consider in terms of assignments including taking a deep look at the role of reading, structuring assignments, managing group work, creating milestones, and providing feedback.

THE ROLE OF READING

Some have asked whether reading is still relevant when it comes to Generation Z. Should everything be on video or involve some sort of entertaining meme or post? While we have discussed in this book many interactive methods for students to learn content outside the scope of reading, it is noteworthy that many in this generation still find reading important. A study by Common Sense Media found that 40 percent of seventeen-year-olds read for fun at least one to two times a week.[245] While that number is down from 52 percent in 2004 and 64 percent in 1985,[246] 86 percent today still believe reading is important to their future.[247]

Although many in Generation Z find reading to be important, they still may not read for class. Consider that Millennials did not spend a lot of time reading in college.[248] So, if Generation Z is similar, instructors may end up dealing with students skimming or not reading altogether as well. Therefore, assigned readings need to foster both engagement and accountability.

AMOUNT OF READING

The old tales about "when we were in school" do not seem to resonate with this age group. Thus, trying to tell them that in college, in particular, it is normal to read hundreds of pages of reading a week for one class may be hard to justify. This nostalgia of "I read this many pages and so should you" might not be the best philosophy. While we want students to read, assigning a lot of reading with the expectation that they retain that content may be unattainable, especially if they are not familiar with academic reading. And before we are quick to say that, for example, forty pages of reading per class per week was not too much for us, we should think again. Did we like that much reading? Did we remember any of the content we read to prepare for a test, even after highlighting nearly every word in the book?

To help determine the right number of pages of reading to assign, consider using the Course Workload Estimator from

Rice University.[249] This tool takes into consideration the purpose and type of each reading when making estimates, and thus recommendations can vary from class to class depending on the reading. While the Course Workload Estimator is focused specifically on reading at the college level, if adjusted, it could also provide insight to determine reading workload for high school students.

FOCUSING READING

To foster deep learning, students need to be able to read for comprehension and not just engage in the mechanics of consuming words on a page.[250] But reading for deep comprehension can take time and cognitive energy. Therefore, it might be helpful to assign one reading for them to deeply focus on rather than several readings that may divide their attention.

INTEGRATING EVERYDAY READINGS

Many educators of older generations went to college during a time in which books and journal articles were the primary sources of information for academic work. Now with more resources, more information, and more technology available, content can come in many written forms, even including shorter print and online pieces in technical and trade journals. These sources, while not always academically rigorous, are often written for everyday readers who want to easily understand subject matter without academic jargon and overly technical explanations. By providing students with a piece written for a general audience paired with a scholarly reading on the same subject, students would have two different, yet complementary, sources to aid in their overall understanding of the topic.

Incorporating Interactive Consumable Content

Perhaps one way to address the issue of information consumption is not how much reading is assigned, but instead the way in which the reading fits into a larger learning experience. In a time in which attention spans are rapidly decreasing,[251] it is critical to ensure that students are engaged in the content. Pearson has introduced an interactive platform designed to replace textbooks.[252] Students can watch videos, do interactive exercises, and simply read less.[253] But what they do read is connected to other interactive ways to better understand and apply that reading.

Utilizing Traditional Reading Formats

With technology today, print is not the only reading format available. Digital books, or e-books, which do not require a physical copy of printed text, are often less expensive and just as available as print copies on sites such as Amazon. While numbers are slightly higher for eighteen- to twenty-nine-year-olds in having read an e-book during the last year, there is not much of a difference when compared with thirty- to forty-nine-year-olds.[254] While some older individuals may be reading e-books, e-book readership is not taking the place of printed text for Generation Z teenagers. For example, in a study of librarians, researchers found that teens have a strong preference for printed books over e-books.[255] So, before moving to e-books, it is important to remember that many Generation Z students may prefer an actual hard-copy.

MAINTAINING STANDARDS OF READING ACCOUNTABILITY

It should be noted that without some type of accountability, Generation Z students may not complete assigned readings. But having either pre-class or in-class assignments related to the assigned readings can help students develop a deeper understanding of the material and ensure they have read for class. For example, have students write a short paper either before or at the beginning of class focused on one of the following:

- Applying the reading (e.g. take one concept from the reading and apply it to a situation in your life right now.)
- Synthesizing the most critical content from the reading (e.g. what are the three most critical points of the reading, and why are those the most critical?)
- Answering a larger question that requires the knowledge of the reading (e.g. given what the authors in the reading said about X, how might policy experts approach Y?)

DEFINING ASSIGNMENT EXPECTATIONS

In addition to aligning reading expectations with Generation Z's preferences and skill sets, it is important to do the same with assignments. Many Generation Z students assert wanting to have well-defined expectations for their learning[256] and "clearly written instructions."[257] Without structure and clarity, there may be frustration among this student cohort. One Generation Z student discussed not wanting her instructors to say, "this what you need to do[;] I don't care how it's done."[258]

While it seems like providing too much structure could constrict their cognitive process, for Generation Z students, though, doing so might simply alleviate anxiety related to correctly completing an assignment. If students do not have to spend mental energy trying to decipher what the instructor wants and are clear about the technical boundaries of the assignment like page length, formatting, and the number of references, they can then focus more time and energy on the content.

SHARING INTENT BEHIND ASSIGNMENTS
Many Generation Z students have an appreciation for the process of learning.[259] Because of this, it may be helpful to have a discussion with them about how and why each assignment was constructed. Doing so could help them see the bigger picture of the goal of the course as well as have greater clarity around the reasoning for certain expectations that may appear arbitrary or at least not as important.

PROVIDING CLEAR INSTRUCTIONS
It may also be helpful to provide resources that can help students with completing assignments. For instance, Generation

Z students would likely appreciate detailed written instructions, checklists, templates, rubrics, and recorded videos they can revisit with tips for completing assignments. Sharing these resources might actually allow them to use their time and energy being inventive with the subject matter rather than attempting to interpret the expectations of their instructors.

SHARING MODEL ASSIGNMENTS

Another strategy for helping Generation Z students better understand expectations involves sharing assignments from past classes that earned an A, ensuring each one is different enough to highlight the diversity of exemplary work. While some instructors may worry that providing a sample assignment might result in limited learning or even academic dishonesty, the reality is that many in Generation Z would rather grapple with their individual content than struggle to figure out how to structure the assignment.

GROUP WORK

Working in groups seems to be a modern-day rite of passage for students—one they cannot escape in most classes today. Whether with one student or several others, the goal is always the same—to complete a large, complex project that would take the human power and diverse perspectives of more than one person.

Today, college classrooms, in particular, are comprised of students from a variety of generations. And while their behavior might be a factor of age or stage in life, each generation brings different approaches to group work. For example, many Baby Boomers in college today are focused on one thing—earning high grades, a sign of both their focus on finishing school and their workaholic mentality.[260] They also like to build relationships with other students and interact face-to-face.[261] Regardless of their busy schedules, they may want to meet with their groups regularly, get to know each of the members, and build connections as part of the group experience.

Gen Xers, on the other hand, see work-life balance as critical.[262] While they will make the time to meet with a group on a regular basis, they will likely not overcommit to completing work in between meetings unless it is solely independent and aligns with their autonomous nature.[263]

Millennials, as collaborative as they are,[264] tend to approach group work as if they were each engaging in a solo project that would eventually be combined with other solo projects to form the final group project. They may even achieve this without meeting, instead dividing the work equally from the beginning and converging at the end to assemble all the pieces.

Generation Z students, will likely meet regularly but work independently next to each other on their assigned piece, reflecting their passion for social learning.[265] This is likely because many in Generation Z do not like working in groups and have found a workaround for doing so—working next to each other rather than working with each other.

In our *Generation Z Goes to College* study, we found that 25 percent believe interpersonal learning is not effective.[266] They expressed three reasons for why they do not prefer interpersonal learning. First, they are concerned about others' ability to follow through when their grades and academic reputation are on the line.[267] Second, they admit that they lack interpersonal skills[268] and, thus, may simply find it difficult to work with others. Finally, some are concerned that they will not be prepared or knowledgeable enough to contribute to a group; they worry that they will need time to learn about the expectations of the project and the content they need so they can be successful—which may take too long to do and hold the group back.[269] One student in our *Generation Z Goes to College* study said, "I also prefer to work alone so I can get a clear understanding of what the purpose of what I'm doing is."[270]

Knowing it is important for Generation Z students to learn how to work in groups, as they will do so in many capacities throughout their lives, the group experience should be structured to be value-added and not detrimental to their learning.

GROUP PROJECT FORMATION

There are many ways to divide students into groups for assignments and projects. They could be randomly assigned, counted out in alphabetical order, grouped by availability (weekends versus evenings), or self-selected by the students. While all methods have their merits, giving students options for how they want to be grouped aligns with Generation

Z's sense of responsibility, especially to make their own choices.[271] Thus, some students may want to form their own groups, whereas others may want to be assigned a group by the instructor.

Many Generation Z students lack a preference for interpersonal learning,[272] so they may at least want their group experiences to involve people they know. Given their characteristics of responsibility and loyalty as well as being motivated by not wanting to let others down,[273] Generation Z students might be perfectly situated to maximize their group experience with those whom they have previous connections. And although there may be benefits for assembling diverse teams where students have different perspectives and life experiences,[274] with Generation Z, familiarity with group members may make it easier for them to tap into their responsibility, loyalty, and self-accountability as well as develop trust and cohesion.[275]

While it might be more efficient to form groups during class, doing so outside of class might work better for Generation Z students. For one, some may not want to form their own groups and instead wait to be assigned by the instructor. Having the group-formation process take place outside of class removes the pressure for these students to join a group during class. And for those who want to form their own groups, it may be helpful to provide time and space outside of class for them to thoughtfully consider their options regarding who they might want to work with rather than feeling rushed on the spot to form a group. And finally, forming groups outside of class removes the awkwardness of students having to select other group members in front of their peers.

GROUP DEVELOPMENT

Without knowing how to work in a group, even the most driven and dedicated students might struggle to work together. As discussed in an earlier chapter, it is important to spend some time during the course to discuss strategies for working in groups, how to handle group conflict, and best practices for effective group functioning. In addition, administering personal assessments, such as the CliftonStrengthsFinder or the Myers-Briggs Type Indicator, offers students an opportunity to enhance their self-awareness while gaining insight into the dynamics of their group. Knowing each other's dispositions, strengths, and preferences can help the students appreciate and leverage the capacities of all group members.

In addition, trust is a critical element of working with a group.[276] Even if students choose their own groups surrounded by others they know does not necessarily mean they have built trusting relationships. So consider incorporating teambuilding into the curriculum as a way to help the group members get to know each other better, develop trust, and enhance their communication.

TEAM CONTRACTS

Research has found that more than 51 percent of Generation Z college seniors report having average or below average levels of social self-confidence.[277] Working in a group may be challenging for those who lack social self-confidence as those students may not readily address issues with their peers when they arise. Therefore, having tools and resources that can aid with group functioning could help students feel more confident to speak up and discuss concerns.

One tool that Generation Z students may find useful for empowering each other to address issues is the team contract. This document is created by the group and lays out the agreed-upon expectations of all group members, such as how frequently they communicate and how they handle issues of conflict and accountability, along with a list of each individual's project responsibilities and deadlines. Having students complete the contract helps ensure that everyone is on the same page going into the project. The contract, however, can also offer group members something to refer to if the contract is not being upheld.

It is helpful for instructors to have a team contract template available that includes a number of common group items that the students might not know to include. For example, "We will use _____ [text, email, social media, etc.] as our primary form of communication" and "All individual components of the project will be completed at least _____ days before the assignment due date so that the group can consolidate the parts and complete final proofing before submission."

MANDATORY GROUP MEETING
To prevent students from approaching group projects as simply a collection of individual parts, it may be important to

require one or more structured group meetings to help them engage in a joint effort from the beginning. Meetings can be done either face-to-face or through a video platform, both mediums they enjoy.[278] For the meeting, each group would be required to gather for a set amount of time and complete an accountability project during the meeting, which could include an outline, a project template, etc. It is important that the meeting is not just a time for students to dole out tasks but more so a time for them to discuss the approach to the project, brainstorm ideas, or grapple with tough questions related to the assignment. In addition, have the students audio record or take detailed notes of the meeting for the instructor to review as a means to ensure the group met and is on track with the project.

WORK DISTRIBUTION

Generation Z students may be drawn to a leaderless group given they more often engage in task execution over leadership.[279] But task allocation must be intentional to maximize group functioning, especially in a group where there may be no leader to step in and ensure tasks are getting done. One method for purposeful task allocation involves using each student's results from the CliftonStrengthsFinder or the Myers-Briggs Type Indicator discussed earlier. For example, a student who has a strength or type involving analysis may be most appropriately matched with tasks related to researching content for the project, whereas another student may excel with detail and might be best suited for editing any writing associated with the project. Without intentional task allocation, however, the group may end up dividing all tasks evenly (e.g. each student writes three pages) or haphazardly (e.g. students volunteer for or are assigned tasks by the group), missing the opportunity to maximize the unique approach each student brings to the project.

INDIVIDUAL CONTRIBUTIONS

Many Generation Z students like to be able to engage in pre-learning before working with others.[280] Doing so helps them develop both knowledge and confidence around course content so they can feel comfortable and informed when asked to share in front of others.[281] Pre-learning, however, does not just benefit the individual students who engage in it. Incorporating opportunities for each student to individually prepare for and contribute to a group project can also be critical for effective team-based learning.[282] For example, having members share well thought-out and unique perspectives from their individual pre-learning experiences offers the group a diverse array of content to consider for the larger group project.

One strategy to infuse an individual pre-learning experience prior to a group project involves having each student complete an assignment related to the project as a primer before they begin working with the group. For instance, ask students to research and write about two advantages and two disadvantages in regard to topic X or three ways to implement topic Y. Once students come together in their groups, they can all share their individual assignments, giving them a starting point for approaching the group project.

ACCOUNTABILITY STANDARDS

It is difficult to imagine anyone wanting to work in a group with a member who lacks follow-through, and Generation Z students are no exception.[283] But because one of the main motivators of Generation Z students involves not letting others down,[284] it is likely that these students also do not want to be those very members that let the group down.

Peer and self-evaluations can be useful for assessing group members' contribution and follow-through. But completing these evaluations after an assignment is due can result in the feedback being more of a grade justification and not a means for improving group functioning. Because Generation Z students do not want to let others down[285] and because the majority of them want feedback on their academic work,[286] it may be more useful to instead have multiple peer and self-evaluation opportunities during the span of the assignment rather than at the end. Doing so would allow students to make any enhancements or changes to their behavior along the way before the project was over.

MILESTONES

Many Generation Z students are motivated by the opportunity for advancement and achieving credit toward something larger[287]—both factors that align with the notion of milestones. Milestones are simply building blocks toward something larger. But how often are students assigned a one-time freestanding project to complete in its entirety, absent any milestones, where feedback is only given after the project is submitted? Probably more often than not. It may be important, not just for sustained engagement in a larger project, but also for student success, to integrate milestones into course assignments.

DIVIDING UP LARGE ASSIGNMENTS

One such strategy for incorporating milestones is to divide larger assignments into smaller ones, with both workload and feedback distributed throughout the process. Instead of assigning a twelve-page paper, perhaps have students write three four-page papers where each has a specific focus that is later woven together for a fourth and final assignment—a twelve-page paper. Not only can dividing up large assignments provide students the opportunity to see their achievements along the way, but doing so also allows instructors to provide feedback that can be integrated into subsequent and culminating assignments.

GAMIFICATION

Another way to incorporate milestones into the curriculum involves using gamification, which is the process of infusing elements from games into nongame contexts to motivate individuals.[288] In the digital world, gamification is embedded in a multitude of apps where users advance levels and carn stars, badges, and tokens as they complete certain tasks. For example, Fitbit, a wearable fitness tracking device, offers users individual and group fitness challenges as well as digital badges for achieving fitness goals.[289] Gamification is also used in nondigital settings as a way to motivate individuals to complete certain tasks. Progress can be measured in a variety of ways including earning reward tokens for achievement or badges for skill acquisition.

One way to infuse gamification in a curricular setting involves awarding badges to students for completing a certain set of assignments. For example, after delivering three presentations, students would earn the public speaking badge. Badge requirements could be limited to the completion of assignments within one course or spread across many. There could also be rewards for badge earnings, where perhaps a certain number of badges or collection of badges earns the student an opportunity to enter a raffle. It is important to note, however, that many Generation Z students do not like competition with others or public recognition,[290] so it is critical that any gamified experiences are self-competitive, and progress is not posted publicly.

PROVIDING FEEDBACK

In a study of Generation Z college seniors, 58 percent reported that they frequently seek feedback on their academic work, and another 38 percent indicated doing so occasionally.[291] Perhaps this is due to Generation Z students being motivated by advancement,[292] craving self-improvement,[293] or having a fear of not living up to their potential.[294] Regardless, feedback is important for them.

TIMELY, THOROUGH, AND ONGOING FEEDBACK

Generation Z students want to know they are on the right track when it comes to meeting course expectations.[295] Because of this, it is important to provide timely, thorough, and ongoing feedback to them. But as instructors, it is easy to let assignments pile up. Getting behind on grading means that if a student makes an error in an early assignment and then unknowingly repeats that error in subsequent assignments, both the student's grade and morale could suffer. Thus, staying on top of grading can help Generation Z students stay on track in the course.

OBSERVATIONAL FEEDBACK

Because many Generation Z students prefer applied and experiential learning, assessing them on the demonstration of tasks, rather than solely on cognitive learning, may be beneficial. Performing a task allows them the opportunity to practice skills and develop confidence, both important factors for Generation Z students when it comes to learning.[296] For example, instead of administering a test or asking students to present on what they know, have students engage in a task, observe them, and then grade them on their demonstration of the executed task. It is not uncommon in subjects that have labs, practicums, or internships to be assessed on the demonstration of tasks. Even the notion of "show your work" in math seems to embrace this approach, where although the answer might be incorrect, the process is accurate. It might be useful to think of ways to infuse task demonstration into courses that may not readily infuse this approach in an effort to provide feedback to students that is process- rather than outcome-oriented.

GENERAL PERFORMANCE FEEDBACK

In addition to assignment feedback, ungraded general performance feedback could also be helpful for student learning and development. Performance feedback can include non-assignment-related factors such as participation, level of inquiry regarding course subject matter, as well as disposition and behavior during class time. This type of feedback could be offered in a number of ways, but a midterm report might be best because it allows the instructor enough time to get to know each student while having adequate time remaining in the course for the student to make any modifications after receiving feedback.

Given that Generation Z students do not appreciate public recognition at all,[297] it is highly unlikely that they would want any type of performance feedback in front of others (even if it was positive). They would likely rather receive feedback in a one-on-one setting where the dialogue would model more of a mentoring meeting than a performance evaluation.

OPPORTUNITIES TO INTEGRATE FEEDBACK

While providing feedback is essential for justifying the grade students are awarded, more importantly, offering feedback gives students the opportunity to make improvements on future assignments. But if students are not required to do anything with the feedback they receive, they may only look at their grade and bypass the great insight shared with them by their instructors. But many in Generation Z like to be able to practice what they learn.[298] Thus, it would be beneficial to provide opportunities for students to resubmit their assignments incorporating instructor feedback. One way to do this would be to award students an initial grade for an assignment and then allow them to resubmit the assignment to earn back up to 50 percent of the points they missed. This way, there is an incentive for students to put forth effort into completing the first submission but also an incentive to resubmit a second updated version.

SUMMARY

When it comes to course assignments, there are some contextual issues and generational preferences that may impact what might work best for student learning. Taking these factors into account, instructors need to consider managing reading expectations, offering clear and detailed assignment instructions, maximizing groups for effective learning, developing milestones, and providing clear, timely, and ongoing feedback.

Conclusion

Generation Z students, much like those in the generations who came before, are eager to learn. But their characteristics, interests, styles, and preferred learning environments are in many ways different from their predecessors. Thus, knowing these factors can be instrumental in designing learning experiences that maximize the potential of this generation to excel in their learning today while rising to the challenges of tomorrow.

Acknowledgments

We are incredibly grateful to the reviewers who gave valuable feedback to us in the writing process. A huge thank-you to the following individuals:

DANIEL M. JENKINS, PhD, is chair and associate professor of leadership and organizational studies at the University of Southern Maine. He received his doctorate in curriculum and instruction as well as an MA in political science from the University of South Florida and a BS in communication studies from Florida State University. Dr. Jenkins is the coauthor of the book *The Role of Leadership Educators: Transforming Learning*, has published more than thirty articles on leadership education and assessment, and is an associate editor for the *Journal of Leadership Studies*.

SHERI STOVER is an associate professor and the program director for the instructional design for digital learning program at Wright State University. She has worked in the field of instructional design in higher education for over twenty years. Sheri earned her PhD in instructional design and has published and presented extensively in the areas of teaching and learning.

Notes

1. Seemiller, C. & Grace, M. (2016). *Generation Z goes to college*. San Francisco: Jossey-Bass.
2. Seemiller, C. & Grace, M. (2019). *Generation Z: A century in the making*. London: Routledge.
3. Purcell, K., Rainie, L., Heaps, A., Buchanan, J., Friedrich, L., Jacklin, A., … Zickuhr, K. (2012). *How teens do research in the digital world*. Retrieved from http://www.pewinternet.org/2012/11/01/how-teens-do-research-in-the-digital-world/
4. Fuentes, G. (2014). Pedagogy with and against the flow: Generational shifts, social media, and the Gen Z brain. In J. Stuart & M. Wilson (Eds.), *102nd ACSA Annual Meeting Proceedings, Globalizing Architecture/ Flows and Disruptions*. Miami Beach, FL: Association of Collegiate Schools of Architecture.
5. Purcell, K., Rainie, L., Heaps, A., Buchanan, J., Friedrich, L., Jacklin, A., … Zickuhr, K. (2012).
6. Purcell, K., Rainie, L., Heaps, A., Buchanan, J., Friedrich, L., Jacklin, A., … Zickuhr, K. (2012).
7. GCF Learnfree.org. (n.d.) *Google search cheat sheet*. Retrieved from https://media.gcflearnfree.org/ctassets/ topics/213/cheat_sheet_search.pdf
8. Wikipedia. (n.d.). *History of Wikipedia*. Retrieved from https://en.m.wikipedia.org/wiki/History_of_ Wikipedia
9. Wikipedia. (n.d.).

10. McAddo, T. (2009). *How to cite Wikipedia in APA style*. Retrieved from https://blog.apastyle.org/apastyle/2009/10/how-to-cite-wikipedia-in-apa-style.html

11. Purcell, K., Rainie, L., Heaps, A., Buchanan, J., Friedrich, L., Jacklin, A., ... Zickuhr, K. (2012).

12. Higher Education Research Institute. (2017). *College Senior Survey*. Data prepared by the Higher Education Research Institute.

13. Cornell University. (n.d.). *Source evaluation checklist*. Retrieved from https://digitalliteracy.cornell.edu/tutorial/SourceEvaluationChecklist.pdf

14. Fink, L. D. (2003). *Creating significant learning experiences*. San Francisco: Jossey-Bass.

15. Purcell, K., Rainie, L., Heaps, A., Buchanan, J., Friedrich, L., Jacklin, A., ... Zickuhr, K. (2012).

16. Macmillan Dictionary. (n.d.). *Critical thinking*. Retrieved from https://www.macmillandictionary.com/us/dictionary/american/critical-thinking

17. Chan, J., Fu, K., Schunn, C., Cagan, J., Wood, K., Kotovsky, K. (2011). On the benefits and pitfalls of analogies for innovative design: Ideation performance based on analogical distance, commonness, and modality. *Journal of Mechanical Design,133*(081004), 1–11. doi: 10.1115/1.4004396

18. World Economic Forum. (2016). *The future of jobs*. Retrieved from http://reports.weforum. org/future-of-jobs-2016/

19. Adobe Educate. (2016). *Gen Z in the classroom: Creating the future*. Retrieved from http://www.adobeeducate. com/genz/adobe-education-genz

20. Adobe Educate. (2016).

21. Adobe Educate. (2016).

22. Higher Education Research Institute. (2017).

23. World Economic Forum. (2016).

24. Land, M. H. (2013). Full STEAM ahead: The benefits of integrating the arts into STEM. *Procedia Computer Science, 20*, 547–552.

25. Higher Education Research Institute. (2017).

26. Parsad, B. Splegelman, M., & Coopersmith, J. (2012). *Arts education in public elementary and secondary schools 1999–2000 and 2009–2010*. Retrieved from http:// nces.ed.gov/ pubs2012/2012014.pdf

27. Adobe Educate. (2016).

28. Whatis.com. (n.d.). *PechaKucha (pecha kucha)*. Retrieved from https://whatis.techtarget.com/definition/PechaKucha-pecha-kucha

29. TED Staff. (2014). *10 tips on how to make slides that communicate your idea, from TED's in-house expert*. Retrieved from https://blog.ted.com/10-tips-for-better-slide-decks/

30. Vidyarthyi, N. (2011). *Attention spans have dropped from 12 to 5 minutes: How social media is ruining our minds*. Retrieved from www.adweek.com/socialtimes/attention-spans-have-dropped-from-12-minutes-to-5-seconds-how-social-media-is-ruiningour-minds-infographic/87484

31. Stover, S. & Seemiller, C. (2017). *Digital distractions study*. Unpublished raw data.

32. Grohol, J. M. (2011). *FOMO addiction: The fear of missing out*. Retrieved from http://psychcentral.com/blog/archives/2011/04/14/fomo-addiction-the-fearof-missing-out/

33. Rosen, L. & Samuel, A. (2015). *Conquering digital distraction*. Retrieved from https://hbr.org/2015/06/conquering-digital-distraction

34. Rosen, L. & Samuel, A. (2015).

35. Mrazek, M. D., Franklin, M. S., Phillips, D. W., Baird, B., & Schooler, J. W. (2012). Mindfulness training improves working memory capacity and GRE performance while reducing mind wandering. *Psychological Science, 24*(5), 776–781.

36. Gazzaley, A. & Rosen, L. D. (2017). *The distracted mind: Ancient brains in a high-tech world*. Cambridge, MA: The MIT Press.

37. Seemiller, C. & Grace, M. (2016).

38. Seemiller, C. & Grace, M. (2016).

39. Ryback, R. (2016). *From Baby Boomers to Generation Z*. Retrieved from www. google.com/amp/s/www.psychologytoday.com/blog/the-truisms-wellness/201602/baby-boomers-generation-z%3Famp

40. Seemiller, C. & Grace, M. (2016).

41. Seemiller, C. & Grace, M. (2016).

42. Kendzior, S. (2014). *Only Baby Boomers could afford to be helicopter parents*. Retrieved from www.theatlantic.

com/business/archive/2014/11/only-baby-boomers-could-afford-to-be-helicopter-parents/382671/

43. Quealy, K. & Cain Miller, C. (2019). *Young adulthood in America: Children are grown, but parenting doesn't stop.* Retrieved from https://www.nytimes.com/2019/03/13/upshot/parenting-new-norms-grown-children-extremes.html?module=inline

44. Graham, B. (2018). *Five big differences between Millennials and Gen Z that you need to know.* Retrieved from https://www.collaborata.com/blog/five-big-differences-between-millennials-and-gen-z-that-you-need-to-know

45. Sparks & Honey. (2014). *Meet Generation Z: Forget everything you learned about Millennials.* Retrieved from https://www.slideshare.net/sparksandhoney/generation-z-final-june-17

46. Altitude. (2017) *Designing Gen Z: 4 insights for powerful generational design.* Retrieved from https://www.altitudeinc.com/designing-for-gen-z/

47. Stillman, D. & Stillman, J. (2017). *Gen Z @ work: How the next generation is transforming the workplace.* New York: HarperCollins.

48. Ologie. (2017). *We are Generation Z.* Retrieved from https://ologie.com/gen-z/#

49. Varkey Foundation. (2017). *Generation Z: Global Citizenship Survey.* Retrieved from www.varkeyfoundation.org/what-we-do/policy-research/generation-z-global-citizenship-survey/

50. Seemiller, C. & Grace, M. (2016).

51. Ologie. (2017).

52. Varkey Foundation. (2017).

53. Seemiller, C. & Grace, M. (2016).

54. Varkey Foundation. (2017).

55. Google.com. (2017). *Generation Z: New insights into the mobile-first mindset of teens.* Retrieved from http://storage.googleapis.com/think/docs/GenZ_Insights_All_teens.pdf

56. Nicol, D., Thomson, A., & Breslin, C. (2014). Rethinking feedback practices in higher education: a peer review perspective. *Assessment & Evaluation in Higher Education, 39*(1), 102–122.

57. Seemiller, C. & Grace, M. (2016).

58. Seemiller, C. & Grace, M. (2017c). *Generation Z stories study.* Unpublished raw data.

59. BridgeWorks. (2017). *Generation X 101.* Retrieved from www.generations.com/ 2017/02/21/generation-x-101/

60. Taylor, P. & Gao, G. (2014). *Generation X: America's neglected "middle child."* Retrieved from www.pewresearch.org/fact-tank/2014/06/05/generation-x-americas-neglected-middle-child/

61. VIA Institute on Character. (2018). *The VIA Survey of character strengths: United States Gen Z.* Data prepared by The VIA Institute on Character.

62. Linnenbrink, E. A. & Pintrich, P. R. (2002). Motivation as an enabler for academic success. *School Psychology Review, 31*(3), 313–327.

63. Seemiller, C. & Grace, M. (2016).

64. Seemiller, C. & Grace, M. (2016).

65. VIA Institute on Character. (2018).

66. Seemiller, C. & Grace, M. (2016).

67. Seemiller, C. & Grace, M. (2016).

68. Seemiller, C. & Grace, M. (2016).

69. Seemiller, C. & Grace, M. (2016).

70. Seemiller, C. & Grace, M. (2016).

71. Seemiller, C. & Grace, M. (2016).

72. Sensis and Think Now Research. (2016). *We are Gen Z report*. Retrieved from http://www.wearegenzreport.com/

73. Higher Education Research Institute. (2017).

74. Zacharia, H. (2019). *Ohio State lab helps students reduce, manage stress*. Retrieved from https://www.dispatch.com/news/20190318/ohio-state-lab-helps-students-reduce-manage-stress

75. Zacharia, H. (2019).

76. Hopler, W. (2017). *Learn a key life skill through the resilience badge workshop*. Retrieved from https://wbu.gmu.edu/learn-a-key-life-skill-through-the-resilience-badge-workshop/

77. Mayor, A. (2018). *USF's public health approach to addressing mental health*. Retrieved from https://hscweb3.hsc.usf.edu/health/publichealth/news/usfs-public-health-approach-to-addressing-mental-health/

78. Quick, J. C. & Henderson, E. F. (2016). Occupational stress: Preventing suffering, enhancing wellbeing. *International Journal of Environmental Research and Public Health, 13*(5), 459.

79. Häfner, A., Stock, A., Pinneker, L., & Ströhle, S. (2013). Stress prevention through a time management

training intervention: An experimental study. *Educational Psychology, 34*(3), 403–416.

80. Seemiller, C. & Grace, M. (2016).

81. Seemiller, C. & Grace, M. (2019).

82. Seemiller, C. & Grace, M. (2017c).

83. Seemiller, C. & Grace, M. (2017c).

84. Seemiller, C. & Grace, M. (2017c).

85. Seemiller, C. & Grace, M. (2017c).

86. Seemiller, C. & Grace, M. (2017c).

87. Seemiller, C. & Grace, M. (2017c).

88. Cheung, J., Davis, T., & Heukaeufer, E. (2017). *Gen Z brand relationships: Authenticity matters.* Retrieved from https://www-01.ibm.com/common/ssi/cgi-bin/ssialias?htmlfid=GBE03855USEN&

89. Seemiller, C. & Grace, M. (2017c).

90. Seemiller, C. & Grace, M. (2017c).

91. Seemiller, C. & Grace, M. (2016).

92. Seemiller, C. & Grace, M. (2016).

93. Seemiller, C. & Grace, M. (2019).

94. Arguel, A., Lockyer, L., Kennedy, G., Lodge, J. M., & Pachman, M. (2018). Seeking optimal confusion: A review on epistemic emotion management in interactive digital learning environments. *Interactive Learning Environments.* doi: 10.1080/10494820.2018.1457544 [e-pub ahead of print].

95. Northeastern University. (2014). *Innovation survey.* Retrieved from www.northeastern.edu/news/2014/11/innovation-imperative-meet-generation-z/

96. Seemiller, C. & Grace, M. (2017c).

97. Reyes, M., Kaeppel, K., & Bjorngard-Basayne, E. (2018). *Memes and GIFs as powerful classroom tools.* Retrieved from https://www.facultyfocus.com/articles/teaching-with-technology-articles/memes-and-gifs-as-powerful-classroom-tools/

98. Seemiller, C. & Grace, M. (2016).

99. Seemiller, C. & Grace, M. (2016).

100. Seemiller, C. & Grace, M. (2019).

101. Seemiller, C. & Grace, M. (2016).

102. Seemiller, C. & Grace, M. (2016).

103. Seemiller, C. & Grace, M. (2016).

104. Rubin, D. (2016). *Wait, how do I write this email?* (n.p.): Author.

105. Seemiller, C. & Grace, M. (2016).

106. Froiland, J. M., Oros, E., Smith, L., & Hirchert, T. (2012). Intrinsic motivation to learn: The nexus between psychological health and academic success. *Contemporary School Psychology, 16,* 91–100.

107. Seemiller, C. & Grace, M. (2019).

108. Froiland, J. M., Oros, E., Smith, L., & Hirchert, T. (2012).

109. Kaur, D. (2018). *How smart class technology is benefiting education sector.* Retrieved from https://www.entrepreneur.com/article/322587

110. Seemiller, C. & Grace, M. (2014). *Generation Z goes to college study.* Unpublished raw data.

111. Seemiller, C. & Grace, M. (2014).

112. Seemiller, C. & Grace, M. (2014).

113. Seemiller, C. & Grace, M. (2014).

114. Noisli.com. (2014). *Home.* Retrieved from https://www.noisli.com/

115. Seemiller, C. & Grace, M. (2014).

116. Seemiller, C. & Grace, M. (2014).

117. Thompson, W. F., Schellenberg, E. G., & Letnic, A. K. (2012). Fast and loud background music disrupts reading comprehension. *Psychology of Music, 40*(6), 700–708.

118. Kampfe, J., Sedlmeier, P., & Renkewitz, F. (2010). The impact of background music on adult listeners: A meta-analysis. *Psychology of Music, 39*(4), 424–448.

119. Thompson, W. F., Schellenberg, E. G., & Letnic, A. K. (2012). p. 701.

120. Thompson, W. F., Schellenberg, E. G., & Letnic, A. K. (2012).

121. Seemiller, C. & Grace, M. (2014).

122. Seemiller, C. & Grace, M. (2014).

123. Seemiller, C. & Grace, M. (2014).

124. Seemiller, C. & Grace, M. (2014).

125. Seemiller, C. & Grace, M. (2014).

126. Seemiller, C. & Grace, M. (2014).

127. Seemiller, C. & Grace, M. (2014).

128. McCoy, B. (2013). Digital distractions in the classroom: Student classroom use of digital devices for non-class related purposes, *Faculty Publications, College of Journalism & Mass Communications. Paper 71.* Retrieved from http://digitalcommons.unl.edu/journalismfacpub/71

129. Sparks & Honey. (2014).

130. Abel, J. P., Buff, C. L., & Burr, S. A. (2016). Social media and the fear of missing out: Scale development and assessment. *Journal of Business & Economics Research, 14*(1), 33–44.

131. Ugar, N. G., & Koc, T. (2015). Time for digital detox: Misuse of mobile technology and phubbing. *Procedia–Social and Behavioral Sciences, 195*(2015), 1022–1031.

132. Seemiller, C. & Stover, S. (2017). Curbing digital distractions in the classroom. *Contemporary Educational Technology, 8*(3), 214–231.

133. Seemiller, C. & Grace, M. (2016).

134. Lorenz, T. (2019). *The hottest chat app for teens is ... Google Docs*. Retrieved from https://www.theatlantic.com/technology/archive/2019/03/hottest-chat-app-teens-google-docs/584857/

135. Seemiller, C. & Stover, S. (2017).

136. Kuznekoff, J. H. & Titsworth, S. (2013). The impact of mobile phone usage on student learning. *Communication Education, 62*(3), 233–252.

137. Cheong, P. H., Shuter, R., & Suwinyattichaiporn, T. (2013). Managing student digital distractions and hyperconnectivity: Communication strategies and challenges for professorial authority. *Communication Education, 65*(2), 272–289.

138. Cheong, P. H., Shuter, R., & Suwinyattichaiporn, T. (2013).

139. Ugar, N. G., & Koc, T. (2015).

140. Miller, M., Berg, H., Cox, D., Carwile, D., Gerber, H., McGuire, M., …Williams, J. (2011). A bird's eye view of an I-phone world: Differing perceptions of cell phone use in academic settings. *Eastern Education Journal, 40*(1), 3–10.

141. Miller, M., Berg, H., Cox, D., Carwile, D., Gerber, H., McGuire, M., …Williams, J. (2011).

142. Miller, M., Berg, H., Cox, D., Carwile, D., Gerber, H., McGuire, M., …Williams, J. (2011).

143. Seemiller, C. & Grace, M. (2019).

144. Seemiller, C. & Grace, M. (2016).

145. Kuznekoff, J. H. & Titsworth, S. (2013).

146. Ugar, N. G., & Koc, T. (2015).

147. Seemiller, C. & Grace, M. (2016).

148. Kamanetz, A. (2015). *How to get students to stop using their cellphones in class.* Retrieved from http://www.npr.org/sections/ed/2015/11/10/453986816/how-to-get-students-to-stop-using-their-cellphones-in-class

149. Cheever, N. A., Rosen, L. D., Carrier, L. M., & Chavez, A. (2014). Out of sight is not out of mind: The impact of restricting wireless mobile device use on anxiety levels among low, moderate and high users. *Computers in Human Behavior, 37*(2014), 290–297.

150. Bazilian, E. (2017). *Infographic: 50% of Gen Z "can't live without YouTube" and other stats that will make you feel old.* Retrieved from www.adweek.com/digital/infographic-50-of-gen-z-cant-live-without-youtube-and-other-stats-that-will-make-you-feel-old/

151. Seemiller, C. & Grace, M. (2016).

152. Seemiller, C. & Grace, M. (2016).
153. Seemiller, C. & Grace, M. (2014).
154. Seemiller, C. & Grace, M. (2016).
155. Seemiller, C. & Grace, M. (2019).
156. Seemiller, C. & Grace, M. (2014).
157. Seemiller, C. & Grace, M. (2019).
158. Seemiller, C. & Grace, M. (2016).
159. Seemiller, C. & Grace, M. (2016).
160. Seemiller, C. & Grace, M. (2014).
161. Seemiller, C. & Grace, M. (2019).
162. Seemiller, C. & Grace, M. (2014).
163. Seemiller, C. & Grace, M. (2014).
164. Seemiller, C. & Grace, M. (2014).
165. Seemiller, C. & Grace, M. (2017a). Generation Z: Educating and engaging the next generation of students. *About Campus, 22*(3), 21–26. p. 23.
166. Seemiller, C. & Grace, M. (2019).
167. Seemiller, C. & Grace, M. (2014).
168. Seemiller, C. & Grace, M. (2014).
169. Seemiller, C. & Grace, M. (2016).
170. Seemiller, C. & Grace, M. (2019).
171. Linnenbrink, E. A. & Pintrich, P. R. (2002).
172. Seemiller, C. & Grace, M. (2016).
173. Seemiller, C. & Grace, M. (2014).
174. Seemiller, C. & Grace, M. (2014).
175. Higher Education Research Institute. (2017).
176. Brown, M. (2017). *What do college students think about safe spaces?* Retrieved from https://lendedu.com/blog/college-students-think-safe-spaces/

177. Seemiller, C. & Grace, M. (2016).

178. Hoeft, M. E. (2012). Why university students don't read: What professors can do to increase compliance. *International Journal for the Scholarship of Teaching and Learning, 6*(2), Article 12.

179. Seemiller, C. & Grace, M. (2019).

180. Seemiller, C. & Grace, M. (2019).

181. Seemiller, C. & Grace, M. (2014).

182. Seemiller, C. & Grace, M. (2019).

183. Seemiller, C. & Grace, M. (2016).

184. Seemiller, C. & Grace, M. (2014).

185. Seemiller, C. & Grace, M. (2016).

186. Seemiller, C. & Grace, M. (2016).

187. Seemiller, C. & Grace, M. (2014).

188. Seemiller, C. & Grace, M. (2017c).

189. Seemiller, C. & Grace, M. (2016).

190. Seemiller, C. & Grace, M. (2016).

191. Seemiller, C. & Grace, M. (2016).

192. Bresman, H. & Rao, V. D. (2017). *A survey of 19 countries shows how Generations X, Y, and Z are—and aren't—different.* Retrieved from https://hbr.org/2017/08/a-survey-of-19-countries-shows-how-generations-x-y-and-z-are-and-arent-different

193. Seemiller, C. & Grace, M. (2014).

194. Seemiller, C. & Grace, M. (2014).

195. Seemiller, C. & Grace, M. (2014).

196. Seemiller, C. & Grace, M. (2016).

197. Adobe Educate. (2016).

198. Seemiller, C. & Grace, M. (2016).
199. Seemiller, C. & Grace, M. (2017a). p. 22.
200. Seemiller, C. & Grace, M. (2016).
201. Boud, D., Cohen, R., & Sampson, J. (2013). *Peer learning in higher education*. Abingdon, Oxon: Routledge.
202. Seemiller, C. & Grace, M. (2016).
203. Seemiller, C. & Grace, M. (2014).
204. Seemiller, C. & Grace, M. (2014).
205. Seemiller, C. & Grace, M. (2014).
206. Seemiller, C. & Grace, M. (2016).
207. Educational Technology and Mobile Learning. (2013). *6 ways to enhance student learning using iMovie*. Retrieved from https://www.educatorstechnology.com/2013/02/6-way-to-enhance-students-learning.html
208. Seemiller, C. & Grace, M. (2019).
209. Young, J. R. (2009). *When professors create social networks for classes, some see a 'Creepy Treehouse.'* Retrieved from https://www.chronicle.com/blogs/wiredcampus/when-professors-create-social-networks-for-classes-some-students-see-a-creepy-treehouse/4176
210. Stoller, E. (2018). *An interview with AI Addyson-Zhang—Entrepreneurial social media educator.* Retrieved from https://www.insidehighered.com/blogs/student-affairs-and-technology/interview-ai-addyson-zhang-entrepreneurial-social-media
211. Osman, M. (2017). *How to use hashtags on every social media network*. Retrieved from https://sproutsocial.com/insights/how-to-use-hashtags/

212. Institute for Health and Human Potential. (n.d.). *What is emotional intelligence?* Retrieved from https://www.ihhp.com/meaning-of-emotional-intelligence, para. 3.

213. Seemiller, C. & Grace, M. (2019).

214. Higher Education Research Institute. (2017).

215. World Economic Forum. (2016).

216. Maguire, R., Egan, A., Hyland, P., & Maguire, P. (2017). Engaging students emotionally: The role of emotional intelligence in predicting cognitive and affective engagement in higher education. *Higher Education Research & Development, 36*(2), 343–357.

217. Payton, J. W., Wardlaw, D. M., Graczyk, P. A., Bloodworth, M. R., Tompsett, C. J., & Weissberg, R. P. (2000). Social and emotional learning: A framework for promoting mental health and reducing risk behaviors in children and youth. *Journal of School Health, 70*(5), 79–185.

218. Snyder, F. J. (2014). Socio-emotional and character development. *Journal of Character Education, 10*(2), 107–127.

219. Shankman, M. L., Allen, S. J., & Haber-Curran, P. (2015). *Emotionally intelligent leadership for students: Facilitation and activity guide* (2nd ed.). San Francisco: Jossey-Bass.

220. Higher Education Research Institute. (2017).

221. Seemiller, C. & Grace, M. (2017c).

222. Seemiller, C. & Grace, M. (2016).

223. Seemiller, C. & Grace, M. (2016).

224. Seemiller, C. & Grace, M. (2017c).

225. Seemiller, C. & Grace, M. (2014).

226. World Economic Forum. (2016).

227. Seemiller, C. & Grace, M. (2017c).

228. Seemiller, C. & Grace, M. (2017c).

229. Seemiller, C. & Grace, M. (2017c).

230. Seemiller, C. & Grace, M. (2016).

231. Seemiller, C. & Grace, M. (2016).

232. Seemiller, C. & Grace, M. (2017c).

233. Seemiller, C. & Grace, M. (2016).

234. Seemiller, C. & Grace, M. (2016).

235. Seemiller, C. & Grace, M. (2016).

236. Seemiller, C. & Grace, M. (2016).

237. Seemiller, C. & Grace, M. (2017b). *Generation Z leads.* (n.p.): Author.

238. Faller, M. B. (2019). *ASU students perform, exhibit and pitch at Change the World.* Retrieved from https://asunow.asu.edu/20190327-sun-devil-life-asu-students-perform-exhibit-and-pitch-change-world?utm_source=linkedin&utm_medium=social&utm_campaign=asu, para. 2.

239. Upwork & Freelancers Union. (2017). *Freelancing in America: 2017.* Retrieved from https://s3-us-west-1.amazonaws.com/adquiro-content-prod/documents/Infographic_UP-URL_2040x1180.pdf

240. Sparks & Honey. (2014).

241. Seemiller, C. & Grace, M. (2016).

242. Gallup & Operation Hope. (2013). *The 2013 Gallup-Hope Index.* Retrieved from www.operationhope.org/images/uploads/Files/2013galluphopereport.pdf

243. Leckart, S. (2012). *The hackathon is on: Pitching and programming the next killer app.* Retrieved from http://www.wired.com/2012/02/ff_hackathons/

244. Paterson, K. (2006). *Real-life literacy: Classroom tools that promote real-world reading and writing.* Markham, Ontario, Canada: Pembroke Publishers Limited.

245. Common Sense Media. (2014). *Children, teens, and reading.* Retrieved from www. commonsensemedia.org/file/csm-childrenteensandreading-2014pdf/download

246. Common Sense Media. (2014).

247. Scholastic. (2016). *Kids and family reading report: 6th edition.* Retrieved from www. scholastic.com/readingreport/files/Scholastic-KFRR-6ed-2017.pdf

248. Roberts, J. C. & Roberts, K. A. (2008). Deep reading, cost/benefit, and the construction of meaning: Enhancing reading comprehension and deep learning in sociology classes. *Teaching Sociology, 36*, 125–140.

249. Barre, E. (2016). *How much should we assign? Estimating out of class workload.* Retrieved from http://cte.rice.edu/blogarchive/2016/07/11/workload

250. Roberts, J. C. & Roberts, K. A. (2008).

251. Vidyarthyi, N. (2011).

252. Schrager, A. & Wang, A. X. (2017). *College textbooks are going the way of Netflix.* Retrieved from https://qz.com/1039404/end-of-textbooks/

253. Schrager, A. & Wang, A. X. (2017).

254. Perrin, A. (2018). *Nearly one-in-five Americans now listen to audiobooks.* Retrieved from https://www.pewresearch.org/fact-tank/2018/03/08/nearly-one-in-five-americans-now-listen-to-audiobooks/

255. Gray, R. & Howard, V. (2017). Young adult use of ebooks: An analysis of public library services and resources. *Public Library Quarterly, 36*(3), 199–212.

256. Seemiller, C. & Grace, M. (2016).

257. Seemiller, C. & Grace, M. (2014).

258. Seemiller, C. & Grace, M. (2019).

259. Seemiller, C. & Grace, M. (2017c).

260. Ryback, R. (2016).

261. McCraw, M. A. & Martindale, T. (2016). *Instructing multi-generational students.* Retrieved from https://paeaonline.org/wp-content/uploads/2016/07/10b-Instructing-Multi-generational-Students.pdf

262. Seemiller, C. & Grace, M. (2019).

263. Kane, S. (2017). *Common characteristics of Generation X professionals.* Retrieved from https://www.thebalance.com/common-characteristics-of-generation-x-professionals-2164682

264. Myers, K. K. & Sadaghiani, K. (2010). Millennials in the workplace: A communication perspective on Millennials' organizational relationships and performance. *Journal of Business and Psychology, 25*(2), 225–238.

265. Seemiller, C. & Grace, M. (2016).

266. Seemiller, C. & Grace, M. (2019).

267. Seemiller, C. & Grace, M. (2014).

268. Seemiller, C. & Grace, M. (2017c).

269. Seemiller, C. & Grace, M. (2017c).

270. Seemiller, C. & Grace, M. (2014).

271. Seemiller, C. & Grace, M. (2016).

272. Seemiller, C. & Grace, M. (2016).

273. Seemiller, C. & Grace, M. (2016).

274. Michaelsen, L. K., Sweet, M. & Parmalee, D. X. (2009). Team-based learning: Small group learning's next big step. In L. K. Michaelsen, M. Sweet, & D. X. Parmalee (Eds.), *New Directions in Teaching and Learning*: No. 116. Team-based learning: Small-group learning's next big step. San Francisco: Wiley Periodicals, Inc.

275. Michaelsen, L. K., Sweet, M. & Parmalee, D. X. (2009).

276. Lencioni, P. M. 2003). The trouble with teamwork. *Leader to Leader, 29*, 35–40.

277. Higher Education Research Institute. (2017).

278. Seemiller, C. & Grace, M. (2019).

279. Seemiller, C. & Grace, M. (2016).

280. Seemiller, C. & Grace, M. (2016).

281. Seemiller, C. & Grace, M. (2016).

282. Michaelsen, L. K., Sweet, M. & Parmalee, D. X. (2009).

283. Seemiller, C. & Grace, M. (2014).

284. Seemiller, C. & Grace, M. (2016).

285. Seemiller, C. & Grace, M. (2016).

286. Higher Education Research Institute. (2017).

287. Seemiller, C. & Grace, M. (2016).

288. Deterding, S., Dixon, D., Khaled, R., & Nacke, L. (2011). From game design elements to gamefulness: Defining gamification. In *The ACM CHI Conference on Human Factors in Computing Systems 2011*, 12–15.

289. Fitbit. (2019). *Why Fitbit?* Retrieved from https://www.fitbit.com/whyfitbit

290. Seemiller, C. & Grace, M. (2016).

291. Higher Education Research Institute. (2017).

292. Seemiller, C. & Grace, M. (2016).

293. Seemiller, C. & Grace, M. (2017c).

294. Seemiller, C. & Grace, M. (2017c).

295. Seemiller, C. & Grace, M. (2016).

296. Seemiller, C. & Grace, M. (2016).

297. Seemiller, C. & Grace, M. (2016).

298. Seemiller, C. & Grace, M. (2016).

REFERENCES

Abel, J. P., Buff, C. L., & Burr, S. A. (2016). Social media and the fear of missing out: Scale development and assessment. *Journal of Business & Economics Research, 14*(1), 33–44.

Adobe Educate. (2016). *Gen Z in the classroom: Creating the future.* Retrieved from http://www.adobeeducate.com/genz/adobe-education-genz

Altitude. (2017) *Designing Gen Z: 4 insights for powerful generational design.* Retrieved from https://www.altitudeinc.com/designing-for-gen-z/

Arguel, A., Lockyer, L., Kennedy, G., Lodge, J. M., & Pachman, M. (2018). Seeking optimal confusion: A review on epistemic emotion management in interactive digital learning environments. *Interactive Learning Environments.* doi: 10.1080/10494820.2018.1457544 [e-pub ahead of print].

Barre, E. (2016). *How much should we assign? Estimating out of class workload.* Retrieved from http://cte.rice.edu/blogarchive/2016/07/11/workload

Bazilian, E. (2017). *Infographic: 50% of Gen Z "can't live without YouTube" and other stats that will make you feel old.* Retrieved from www.adweek.com/digital/infographic-50-of-gen-z-cant-live-without-youtube-and-other-stats-that-will-make-you-feel-old/

Boud, D., Cohen, R., & Sampson, J. (2013). *Peer learning in higher education.* Abingdon, Oxon: Routledge.

Bresman, H. & Rao, V. D. (2017). *A survey of 19 countries shows how Generations X, Y, and Z are—and aren't—different.*

Retrieved from https://hbr.org/2017/08/a-survey-of-19-countries-shows-how-generations-x-y-and-z-are-and-arent-different

BridgeWorks. (2017). *Generation X 101*. Retrieved from www.generations.com/ 2017/02/21/generation-x-101/

Brown, M. (2017). *What do college students think about safe spaces?* Retrieved from https://lendedu.com/blog/college-students-think-safe-spaces/

Chan, J., Fu, K., Schunn, C., Cagan, J., Wood, K., Kotovsky, K. (2011). On the benefits and pitfalls of analogies for innovative design: Ideation performance based on analogical distance, commonness, and modality. *Journal of Mechanical Design,133*(081004), 1–11. doi: 10.1115/1.4004396

Cheever, N. A., Rosen, L. D., Carrier, L. M., & Chavez, A. (2014). Out of sight is not out of mind: The impact of restricting wireless mobile device use on anxiety levels among low, moderate and high users. *Computers in Human Behavior, 37*(2014), 290–297.

Cheong, P. H., Shuter, R., & Suwinyattichaiporn, T. (2013). Managing student digital distractions and hyperconnectivity: Communication strategies and challenges for professorial authority. *Communication Education, 65*(2), 272–289.

Cheung, J., Davis, T., & Heukaeufer, E. (2017). *Gen Z brand relationships: Authenticity matters.* Retrieved from https://www-01.ibm.com/common/ssi/cgi-bin/ssialias?htmlfid=GBE03855USEN&

Common Sense Media. (2014). *Children, teens, and reading*. Retrieved from www. commonsensemedia.org/file/csm-childrenteensandreading-2014pdf/download

Cornell University. (n.d.). *Source evaluation checklist*. Retrieved from https://digitalliteracy.cornell.edu/tutorial/SourceEvaluationChecklist.pdf

Deterding, S., Dixon, D., Khaled, R., & Nacke, L. (2011). From game design elements to gamefulness: Defining gamification. In *The ACM CHI Conference on Human Factors in Computing Systems 2011*, 12–15.

Educational Technology and Mobile Learning. (2013). *6 ways to enhance student learning using iMovie*. Retrieved from https://www.educatorstechnology.com/2013/02/6-way-to-enhance-students-learning.html

Faller, M. B. (2019). *ASU students perform, exhibit and pitch at Change the World*. Retrieved from https://asunow.asu.edu/20190327-sun-devil-life-asu-students-perform-exhibit-and-pitch-change-world?utm_source=linkedin&utm_medium=social&utm_campaign=asu

Fink, L. D. (2003). *Creating significant learning experiences*. San Francisco: Jossey-Bass.

Fitbit. (2019). *Why Fitbit?* Retrieved from https://www.fitbit.com/whyfitbit

Froiland, J. M., Oros, E., Smith, L., & Hirchert, T. (2012). Intrinsic motivation to learn: The nexus between psychological health and academic success. *Contemporary School Psychology, 16*, 91–100.

Fuentes, G. (2014). Pedagogy with and against the flow: Generational shifts, social media, and the Gen Z brain. In J. Stuart & M. Wilson (Eds.), *102nd ACSA Annual Meeting Proceedings, Globalizing Architecture/ Flows and Disruptions*. Miami Beach, FL: Association of Collegiate Schools of Architecture.

Gallup & Operation Hope. (2013). *The 2013 Gallup-Hope Index*. Retrieved from www.operationhope.org/images/uploads/Files/2013galluphopereport.pdf

Gazzaley, A. & Rosen, L. D. (2017). *The distracted mind: Ancient brains in a high-tech world*. Cambridge, MA: The MIT Press.

GCF Learnfree.org. (n.d.) *Google search cheat sheet*. Retrieved from https://media.gcflearnfree.org/ctassets/topics/213/cheat_sheet_search.pdf

Google.com. (2017). *Generation Z: New insights into the mobile-first mindset of teens*. Retrieved from http://storage.googleapis.com/think/docs/GenZ_Insights_All_teens.pdf

Graham, B. (2018). *Five big differences between Millennials and Gen Z that you need to know*. Retrieved from https://www.collaborata.com/blog/five-big-differences-between-millennials-and-gen-z-that-you-need-to-know

Gray, R. & Howard, V. (2017). Young adult use of ebooks: An analysis of public library services and resources. *Public Library Quarterly, 36*(3), 199–212.

Grohol, J. M. (2011). *FOMO addiction: The fear of missing out*. Retrieved from http://psychcentral.com/blog/archives/2011/04/14/fomo-addiction-the-fearof-missing-out/

Häfner, A., Stock, A., Pinneker, L., & Ströhle, S. (2013). Stress prevention through a time management training intervention: An experimental study. *Educational Psychology, 34*(3), 403–416.

Higher Education Research Institute. (2017). *College Senior Survey.* Data prepared by the Higher Education Research Institute.

Hoeft, M. E. (2012) Why university students don't read: What professors can do to increase compliance. *International Journal for the Scholarship of Teaching and Learning, 6*(2), Article 12.

Hopler, W. (2017). *Learn a key life skill through the resilience badge workshop.* Retrieved from https://wbu.gmu.edu/learn-a-key-life-skill-through-the-resilience-badge-workshop/

Institute for Health and Human Potential. (n.d.). *What is emotional intelligence?* Retrieved from https://www.ihhp.com/meaning-of-emotional-intelligence

Kamanetz, A. (2015). *How to get students to stop using their cellphones in class.* Retrieved from http://www.npr.org/sections/ed/2015/11/10/453986816/how-to-get-students-to-stop-using-their-cellphones-in-class

Kampfe, J., Sedlmeier, P., & Renkewitz, F. (2010). The impact of background music on adult listeners: A meta-analysis. *Psychology of Music, 39*(4), 424–448.

Kane, S. (2017). *Common characteristics of Generation X professionals.* Retrieved from https://www.thebalance.com/common-characteristics-of-generation-x-professionals-2164682

Kaur, D. (2018). *How smart class technology is benefiting education sector.* Retrieved from https://www.entrepreneur.com/article/322587

Kendzior, S. (2014). *Only Baby Boomers could afford to be helicopter parents.* Retrieved from www.theatlantic.com/business/archive/2014/11/only-baby-boomers-could-afford-to-be-helicopter-parents/382671/

Kuznekoff, J. H. & Titsworth, S. (2013). The impact of mobile phone usage on student learning. *Communication Education, 62*(3), 233–252.

Land, M. H. (2013). Full STEAM ahead: The benefits of integrating the arts into STEM. *Procedia Computer Science, 20*, 547–552.

Leckart, S. (2012). *The hackathon is on: Pitching and programming the next killer app.* Retrieved from http://www.wired.com/2012/02/ff_hackathons/

Lencioni, P. M. 2003). The trouble with teamwork. *Leader to Leader, 29*, 35–40.

Linnenbrink, E. A. & Pintrich, P. R. (2002). Motivation as an enabler for academic success. *School Psychology Review, 31*(3), 313–327.

Lorenz, T. (2019). *The hottest chat app for teens is…Google Docs.* Retrieved from https://www.theatlantic.com/technology/archive/2019/03/hottest-chat-app-teens-google-docs/584857/

Macmillan Dictionary. (n.d.). *Critical thinking.* Retrieved from https://www.macmillandictionary.com/us/dictionary/american/critical-thinking

Maguire, R., Egan, A., Hyland, P., & Maguire, P. (2017). Engaging students emotionally: The role of emotional intelligence in predicting cognitive and affective engagement in higher education. *Higher Education Research & Development, 36*(2), 343–357.

Mayor, A. (2018). *USF's public health approach to addressing mental health.* Retrieved from https://hscweb3.hsc.usf.edu/health/publichealth/news/usfs-public-health-approach-to-addressing-mental-health/

McAddo, T. (2009). *How to cite Wikipedia in APA style.* Retrieved from https://blog.apastyle.org/apastyle/2009/10/how-to-cite-wikipedia-in-apa-style.html

McCoy, B. (2013). Digital distractions in the classroom: Student classroom use of digital devices for non-class related purposes, *Faculty Publications, College of Journalism & Mass Communications. Paper 71.* Retrieved from http://digitalcommons.unl.edu/journalismfacpub/71

McCraw, M. A. & Martindale, T. (2016). *Instructing multi-generational students.* Retrieved from https://pae-aonline.org/wp-content/uploads/2016/07/10b-Instructing-Multi-generational-Students.pdf

Michaelsen, L. K., Sweet, M. & Parmalee, D. X. (2009). Team-based learning: Small group learning's next big step. In L. K. Michaelsen, M. Sweet, & D. X. Parmalee (Eds.), *New Directions in Teaching and Learning*: No. 116. Team-based learning: Small-group learning's next big step. San Francisco: Wiley Periodicals, Inc.

Miller, M., Berg, H., Cox, D., Carwile, D., Gerber, H., McGuire, M., … Williams, J. (2011). A bird's eye view of an I-phone world: Differing perceptions of cell phone use in academic settings. *Eastern Education Journal, 40*(1), 3–10.

Mrazek, M. D., Franklin, M. S., Phillips, D. W., Baird, B., & Schooler, J. W. (2012). Mindfulness training improves working memory capacity and GRE performance while reducing mind wandering. *Psychological Science, 24*(5), 776–781.

Myers, K. K. & Sadaghiani, K. (2010). Millennials in the workplace: A communication perspective on Millennials' organizational relationships and performance. *Journal of Business and Psychology, 25*(2), 225–238.

Nicol, D., Thomson, A., & Breslin, C. (2014). Rethinking feedback practices in higher education: a peer review perspective. *Assessment & Evaluation in Higher Education, 39*(1), 102–122.

Noisli.com. (2014). *Home.* Retrieved from https://www.noisli.com/

Northeastern University. (2014). *Innovation survey.* Retrieved from www.northeastern.edu/news/2014/11/innovation-imperative-meet-generation-z/

Ologie. (2017). *We are Generation Z.* Retrieved from https://ologie.com/gen-z/#

Osman, M. (2017). *How to use hashtags on every social media network.* Retrieved from https://sproutsocial.com/insights/how-to-use-hashtags/

Parsad, B. Splegelman, M., & Coopersmith, J. (2012). *Arts education in public elementary and secondary schools*

1999–2000 and 2009–2010. Retrieved from http://nces. ed.gov/ pubs2012/2012014.pdf

Paterson, K. (2006). *Real-life literacy: Classroom tools that promote real-world reading and writing*. Markham, Ontario, Canada: Pembroke Publishers Limited.

Payton, J. W., Wardlaw, D. M., Graczyk, P. A., Bloodworth, M. R., Tompsett, C. J., & Weissberg, R. P. (2000). Social and emotional learning: A framework for promoting mental health and reducing risk behaviors in children and youth. *Journal of School Health, 70*(5), 79–185.

Perrin, A. (2018). *Nearly one-in-five Americans now listen to audiobooks*. Retrieved from https://www.pewresearch.org/ fact-tank/2018/03/08/nearly-one-in-five-americans-now-listen-to-audiobooks/

Purcell, K., Rainie, L., Heaps, A., Buchanan, J., Friedrich, L., Jacklin, A., … Zickuhr, K. (2012). *How teens do research in the digital world*. Retrieved from http:// www.pewinternet.org/2012/11/01/how-teens-do-research-in-the-digital-world/

Quealy, K. & Cain Miller, C. (2019). *Young adulthood in America: Children are grown, but parenting doesn't stop*. Retrieved from https://www.nytimes.com/2019/03/13/ upshot/parenting-new-norms-grown-children-extremes. html?module=inlineQuick, J. C. & Henderson, E. F. (2016). Occupational stress: Preventing suffering, enhancing wellbeing. *International Journal of Environmental Research and Public Health, 13*(5), 459.

Reyes, M., Kaeppel, K., & Bjorngard-Basayne, E. (2018). *Memes and GIFs as powerful classroom tools*. Retrieved from https://www.facultyfocus.com/articles/teaching-with-technology-articles/memes-and-gifs-as-powerful-classroom-tools/

Roberts, J. C. & Roberts, K. A. (2008). Deep reading, cost/benefit, and the construction of meaning: Enhancing reading comprehension and deep learning in sociology classes. *Teaching Sociology, 36*, 125–140.

Rosen, L. & Samuel, A. (2015). *Conquering digital distraction*. Retrieved from https://hbr.org/2015/06/conquering-digital-distraction

Rubin, D. (2016). *Wait, how do I write this email?* (n.p.): Author.

Ryback, R. (2016). *From Baby Boomers to Generation Z*. Retrieved from www. google.com/amp/s/www.psy-chologytoday.com/blog/the-truisms-wellness/201602/baby-boomers-generation-z%3Famp

Scholastic. (2016). *Kids and family reading report: 6th edition*. Retrieved from www. scholastic.com/readingreport/files/Scholastic-KFRR-6ed-2017.pdf

Schrager, A. & Wang, A. X. (2017). *College textbooks are going the way of Netflix*. Retrieved from https://qz.com/1039404/end-of-textbooks/

Seemiller, C. & Grace, M. (2014). *Generation Z goes to college study*. Unpublished raw data.

Seemiller, C. & Grace, M. (2016). *Generation Z goes to college*. San Francisco: Jossey-Bass.

Seemiller, C. & Grace, M. (2017a). Generation Z: Educating and engaging the next generation of students. *About Campus, 22*(3), 21–26.

Seemiller, C. & Grace, M. (2017b). *Generation Z leads.* (n.p.): Author.

Seemiller, C. & Grace, M. (2017c). *Generation Z stories study.* Unpublished raw data.

Seemiller, C. & Grace, M. (2019). *Generation Z: A century in the making.* London: Routledge.

Seemiller, C. & Stover, S. (2017). Curbing digital distractions in the classroom. *Contemporary Educational Technology, 8*(3), 214–231.

Sensis and Think Now Research. (2016). *We are Gen Z report.* Retrieved from http://www.wearegenzreport.com/

Shankman, M. L., Allen, S. J., & Haber-Curran, P. (2015). *Emotionally intelligent leadership for students: Facilitation and activity guide* (2nd ed.). San Francisco: Jossey-Bass.

Snyder, F. J. (2014). Socio-emotional and character development. *Journal of Character Education, 10*(2), 107–127.

Sparks & Honey. (2014). *Meet Generation Z: Forget everything you learned about Millennials.* Retrieved from www.slideshare.net/sparksandhoney/generation-z-final-june-17

Stillman, D. & Stillman, J. (2017). *Gen Z @ work: How the next generation is transforming the workplace.* New York: HarperCollins.

Stoller, E. (2018). *An interview with AI Addyson-Zhang—Entrepreneurial social media educator.* Retrieved from https://www.insidehighered.com/blogs/student-affairs-and-technology/interview-ai-addyson-zhang-entrepreneurial-social-media

Stover, S. & Seemiller, C. (2017). *Digital distractions study.* Unpublished raw data.

Taylor, P. & Gao, G. (2014). *Generation X: America's neglected "middle child."* Retrieved from www.pewresearch.org/fact-tank/2014/06/05/generation-x-americas-neglected-middle-child/

TED Staff. (2014). *10 tips on how to make slides that communicate your idea, from TED's in-house expert.* Retrieved from https://blog.ted.com/10-tips-for-better-slide-decks/

Thompson, W. F., Schellenberg, E. G., & Letnic, A. K. (2012). Fast and loud background music disrupts reading comprehension. *Psychology of Music, 40*(6), 700–708, p. 701.

Ugar, N. G., & Koc, T. (2015). Time for digital detox: Misuse of mobile technology and phubbing. *Procedia–Social and Behavioral Sciences, 195*(2015), 1022–1031.

Upwork & Freelancers Union. (2017). *Freelancing in America: 2017.* Retrieved from https://s3-us-west-1.amazonaws.com/adquiro-content-prod/documents/Infographic_UP-URL_2040x1180.pdf

Varkey Foundation. (2017). *Generation Z: Global Citizenship Survey.* Retrieved from www.varkeyfoundation.org/what-we-do/policy-research/generation-z-global-citizenship-survey/

VIA Institute on Character. (2018). *The VIA Survey of character strengths: United States Gen Z.* Data prepared by The VIA Institute on Character.

Vidyarthyi, N. (2011). *Attention spans have dropped from 12 to 5 minutes: How social media is ruining our minds.*

Retrieved from http://www.adweek.com/socialtimes/ attention-spans-have-dropped-from-12-minutes-to-5-seconds-how-social-media-is-ruiningour-minds-info-graphic/87484

Whatis.com. (n.d.). *PechaKucha (pecha kucha)*. Retrieved from https://whatis.techtarget.com/definition/PechaKucha-pecha-kucha

Wikipedia. (n.d.). *History of Wikipedia*. Retrieved from https://en.m.wikipedia.org/wiki/History_of_Wikipedia

World Economic Forum. (2016). *The future of jobs*. Retrieved from http://reports.weforum. org/future-of-jobs-2016/

Young, J. R. (2009). *When professors create social networks for classes, some see a 'Creepy Treehouse.'* Retrieved from https://www.chronicle.com/blogs/wiredcampus/when-professors-create-social-networks-for-classes-some-stu-dents-see-a-creepy-treehouse/4176

Zacharia, H. (2019). *Ohio State lab helps students reduce, manage stress*. Retrieved from https://www.dispatch.com/news/20190318/ohio-state-lab-helps-students-reduce-manage-stress

INDEX

Applied Learning, 60-61,
    101-103
Assignment Expectations,
    91-93
Attention Spans, 13-15, 89-90

Choice in Learning, 58-60,
    95-97
Classroom Expectations and
    Standards, 39-41, 52-53,
    64, 91-92
Clear Instructions, 61, 92-93
Communication, 36-41, 66,
    94, 99
    Email, 37-41
    Face-to-Face, 36, 66, 94,
        99
    Text, 36-37
Confidence, 63-64, 97-98, 100
Creativity, 9-13
Critical Thinking, 7-9

Deep Learning, 89
Demonstrated Learning, 68-70
Digital Learning, 70-73
Digital Portfolios, 12-13

Emotional Intelligence, 75-77
Experiential Learning, 67-68

Family Role, 17-20, 26
Feedback, 21, 65, 68-69,
    101-106
    Integrating, 105-106
    Observational, 104-105
    Peer, 21, 68
    Performance, 105
    Timely, Thorough, and
        Ongoing, 104
Flipped Learning, 61-63, 100

Gamification, 102-103
Group Work, 24-25, 59, 72,
    77-78, 93-101
Guest Speakers, 22

Information, 1-7, 62, 89-90
    Overload, 1-3
    Credible, 3-7
Instructors, 31-43
    Characteristics, 32-35
    Creating Connections,
        35-36

Not Letting Down, 41-43
Relationships, 42
Intrapersonal Learning, 57-65

Learning Apps and Platforms, 36, 55, 69-71, 90
Learning Environments, 45-50
Comfortable, 47-50
Outdoor, 49-50
Quiet, 46-47

Milestones, 60-61, 101-103
Mindfulness, 14-15
Model Assignments, 93

Online and Hybrid Courses, 36, 66
Other Generations, 3-4, 17-19, 24, 88, 94
Baby Boomers, 94
Generation X, 17-19, 24, 94
Millennials, 3-4, 17-18, 88, 94

Pacing, 60-61
Parents, 17-20
Co-pilot, 19
Helicopter, 18
Lawnmower, 18

Role of in Learning, 19-20
Peers, 11-12, 20-22, 67-68, 97-98, 101
Facilitation, 11-12, 68
Feedback, 21, 101
Role of in Learning, 21-22, 68, 97-98
Support and Assistance, 22, 67
Presentations, 10-11, 71, 78
Problem-solving, 8, 68, 76, 79

Reading, 3, 47, 59-60, 63, 72, 78, 87-91
Amount, 88-89
Selection, 3, 59-60
Vetted, 3
Researching Online, 1-7, 55, 63, 77-78

Skills, 8, 36, 38, 41, 68, 75-80, 104
Academic, 78
Professional, 79-80
Success, 77
Social and Emotional Learning, 76
Social Change, 80-85

Social Learning, 65-67, 94

Social Media, 4, 51, 53, 58, 71-73, 75

STEAM/STEM, 10

Stress and Wellbeing, 28-29

Students, 23-29
    Characteristics, 23-24
    Motivations, 24-28
    Strengths, 24

Technology, 13-14, 35-36, 47, 50-55, 70-73
    Creating Boundaries, 50-55
    Distractions, 13, 47, 53
    In the Classroom, 35-36
    Unplugging, 13-14

Unlearning, 6-7

Video-Based Learning, 55, 60, 62, 69-70, 90, 93, 99

Wikipedia, 3-4

Made in the USA
Columbia, SC
04 January 2023